Working with Co-Parents

Working with Co-Parents is a practical manual for therapists and social workers who work with divorced and/or separated parents of children. Unique among other books that focus on therapy with the parents individually, the author's model brings the divorced couple together to help them understand their child's experience and to assist them in developing a road to constructive co-parenting. This manual also includes illustrative case vignettes, session outlines and handouts, and homework reflection questions. Therapists and counselors will learn tools and interventions that they can apply immediately and effectively to their work with divorced couples.

Mary L. Jeppsen, PhD, LMFT, is a licensed marriage and family therapist and licensed professional counselor who co-owns Fresh Roots Family Counseling in Rogers, Arkansas. She developed a co-parenting counseling model with the intention of assisting parents in developing healthy co-parenting relationships. Dr. Jeppsen is also a certified Daring Way™ facilitator in the work of Brené Brown.

Working with Co-Parents
A Manual for Therapists

Mary L. Jeppsen

NEW YORK AND LONDON

First edition published 2018
by Routledge
711 Third Avenue, New York, NY 10017

and by Routledge
2 Park Square, Milton Park, Abingdon, Oxon, OX14 4RN

Routledge is an imprint of the Taylor & Francis Group, an informa business

© 2018 Taylor & Francis

The right of Mary L. Jeppsen to be identified as the author of this work has been asserted by her in accordance with sections 77 and 78 of the Copyright, Designs and Patents Act 1988.

All rights reserved. The purchase of this copyright material confers the right on the purchasing institution to photocopy or download pages which bear the photocopy icon and a copyright line at the bottom of the page. No other parts of this book may be reprinted or reproduced or utilized in any form or by any electronic, mechanical, or other means, now known or hereafter invented, including photocopying and recording, or in any information storage or retrieval system, without permission in writing from the publishers.

Trademark notice: Product or corporate names may be trademarks or registered trademarks, and are used only for identification and explanation without intent to infringe.

Library of Congress Cataloging-in-Publication Data
Names: Jeppsen, Mary L., author.
Title: Working with co-parents : a manual for therapists / Mary Jeppsen.
Description: New York : Routledge, 2017. | Includes bibliographical references and index.
Identifiers: LCCN 2017029005| ISBN 9781138240506 (hbk. : alk. paper) | ISBN 9781138240513 (pbk. : alk. paper) | ISBN 9781315283494 (ebk.)
Subjects: | MESH: Family Therapy—methods | Divorce—psychology | Child Rearing—psychology | Family Conflict—psychology | Single-Parent Family—psychology
Classification: LCC RC455.4.F3 | NLM WM 430.5.F2 | DDC 616.89/156—dc23
LC record available at https://lccn.loc.gov/2017029005

ISBN: 978-1-138-24050-6 (hbk)
ISBN: 978-1-138-24051-3 (pbk)
ISBN: 978-1-315-28349-4 (ebk)

Typeset in Galliard
by Swales & Willis Ltd, Exeter, Devon, UK

Contents

	Acknowledgments	vii
	Introduction	ix
	Skillset Required for the Work	xvii
	How to Use This Book	xxi
1	This Is Not Post-Divorce Therapy	1
2	It's About the Children Now	15
3	The Games We Play	33
4	Out of Conflict into Compromise	59
5	Including Step-Parents in the Process	73
6	Each Parent Needs a Voice	77
7	Developing the Co-Parenting Plan	81
8	The Final Family Session	89
9	Therapeutic and Ethical Challenges	93
	Further Study	97
	Bibliography	99
	Index	103

Acknowledgments

I am grateful to my husband, Michael, for his support, and to my children: Tina, Jonathan, Bethany, Matthew, Rebecca, Christian, Mary, Abigail, Hannah, Elizabeth, and Serah, for believing in their Mom.

I want to acknowledge Lacey Sherrill LCMSW and Rebecca Zeleny LCMSW for sharing their ideas with me a long time ago, and for granting me permission to use them in my work.

Most of all I am thankful to the parents and children of Benton County who have entrusted their relationships to me, and to the Family Court Judges of Benton and Washington County, Arkansas, for trusting me to work with their people.

Introduction

Divorce is with us. In both popular literature and scholarly publications the consensus is that the divorce rate in the United States is between 40% and 50%, which means that 40–50% of the children born to families in the United States will have to cope with and adjust to divorce (www.apa.org/topics/divorce).

Also, that rate increases as people remarry, where the second marriage is even more likely to dissolve into divorce.

In my private practice, I began as a play therapist and then a marital counselor. I spent years in the schools and in my practice working with children who were from families that were breaking or broken. These children were often caught in the middle between parents who were having grave difficulty in their marriages. Work with the children was often frustrating because the children were so tuned in to their parents' struggles, and I could not effect change without dealing with the whole family system. So, I began to work with couples, hoping to make a difference and provide some help indirectly for the children. My orientation in couples work is Emotion-Focused Couples Therapy (Greenburg and Johnson, 2010). I used attachment theory and concentrated upon renewing emotional bonds between parents and spouses. In this Emotion-Focused work, it became clear to me that attachment is essential to emotional health.

Four years ago, I had a revelation. The children that I was seeing and that my colleagues were seeing, who had experienced the divorce of their parents, seemed to have a pattern. No matter how long ago their parents' divorce had taken place, the children of these families would present with challenges when their parents were litigating. The children whose parents were embroiled in custody battles seemed to be having great difficulty. They were presenting as being emotionally healthy or unhealthy in conjunction with the relative health of their biological parents' relationship. In addition, often the parents would attempt to use me and my colleagues to obtain custody. They asked for our testimony in court. This put us in an untenable situation, as we are not custody evaluators. We are counselors. These custody battles were some of the most challenging cases because seeing the child often did not help the parental relationship, and most divorced people did not want to visit with us together. It resulted in a "he said, she said" situation. All the while I became more and more concerned about the disrupted attachment experienced by the children of divorce.

Dr. Edward Farber, in his book *Raising the Kid You Love With the Ex You Hate* (2013), states that there is a direct correlation between a child's adjustment to divorce and the civility with which the parents treat each other. I have found in my practice that this is true and that this is not as much dependent upon the "age" of the divorce, but on the relationship of the parents. In other words, even if a parent has been divorced for 15 years, if he or she has an acrimonious relationship with their ex, the child will be adversely affected and have difficulty adjusting. I have seen divorced couples that have been divorced for over 11 years who continued to fight over issues related to their children. The children were reacting to the disruption of their secure base (their parents' relationship).

As a result of dealing with custody issues and post-marital conflict, I began to rethink how to approach divorced families. Historically, a child would be presented as the Identified Patient, and I would do play therapy and then include Mom and Dad separately in the therapy process. It was frustrating because the parents often parented their children very differently from each other. And this imbalance encouraged an unhealthy dynamic in the children, who seemed to be juggling two sets of emotions: Dads' emotions and Mom's emotions.

Divorce is an incredibly emotional experience. Two people who have been woven together are unraveling their lives. It is messy and it is painful, even if it is warranted. When the idea of parenting with the ex-spouse is introduced, the messiness multiplies. In my practice the children that I was seeing were the ones caught between two hurting people. These wounded people were being asked by the court to do the most difficult task of their lives, together with someone that they could not get along with, did not see eye to eye with, and often hated. This most difficult task is parenting. I began to explore the idea that parenting together after divorce must be nearly impossible without some help and guidance. I researched the written materials, and there are several very good books (see the Bibliography) on how to navigate divorce and co-parenting.

These are written for parents who want to do well parenting after divorce. I saw that there are group programs to educate divorced people. These group programs are the norm. But these did not seem completely effective, especially for those parents who have great difficulty parenting together. It seemed to me that people can hold their breath and play on their phones in a group class, with no personal investment or challenge. People in high-conflict divorces are generally stuck in such a negative interaction cycle that a group will not break through the pattern. My Emotion-Focused Therapy training taught me that de-escalation of the negative pattern is essential for relational health, so I began to wonder how I could assist these couples in de-escalation when there was no connection, and where it was not advisable to keep emotional connections.

Most divorced people who do well in parenting together are those who are motivated to read the books and attend the groups. But what about those parents who are so hurt and angry that they cannot? These were the parents that I saw in my office often. And these were the parents who could not navigate parenting together. There was no program mandated in my state (Arkansas) that would help the couple face their negative patterns personally in a safe environment. The only alternative was personal reading of "how-to" books and attending group classes. So, I developed a program. Interestingly, as I have developed the program I have found that even the seemingly civil divorced people have trouble parenting together. Actually, married people have trouble parenting together. Why should it be any different for divorced people?

I approached the Benton County Arkansas Family Court judges with my idea. These judges seemed to be in a quandary when awarding joint custody, because often couples would litigate several times after the original divorce decree and custody settlement. This was understandably frustrating to the court. I offered a personal program to both educate and support divorced and divorcing couples, which would shift their focus off themselves and their own hurt onto their children who were being negatively affected by their conflict and litigious lifestyles. That was almost four years ago. These couples make up over 50% of my practice. I count it an honor to help these parents navigate what I would say is the most difficult challenge of their lives. I see it as family work and as protective work for the children.

My background is in play therapy. Play therapy, like Emotion-Focused Couples Therapy, emphasizes attachment. Attachment is at the base of all safety and security. The work of John Bowlby et al. (1986)

bears this out. Attachment is what is directly threatened in a high-conflict divorce situation. Children lose their secure base when Mom and Dad separate and the child is suddenly living in two worlds. Safety and security are the most essential elements of a child's life and these are threatened when parents divorce. Safety and security are the essential elements that provide children an atmosphere in which to learn and grow.

Dr. Robert E. Emery (2016) has developed a hierarchy of needs for children of divorce. In this hierarchy, survival and safety are at the base. Divorce directly attacks a child's sense of safety and security. When attachment is disrupted, children react. In the chaos that divorce often brings, sometimes children's feelings are not at the forefront. I wanted to somehow reach parents where they attach to their children, where they are still loving someone, so that post-divorce they can transform their pain into concern for those whom they truly love and are committed to. This might be the key to renewing safety, security, and secure attachment.

This is a particular challenge because divorce is the dissolution of a very strong attachment. Divorce in itself needs an attachment to die. But in the face of this there are children who cannot bear the death of attachment. It is a dichotomy that has to be faced and navigated if children are to have normal childhoods. As Dr. Emery (2016) says, every child must be able to have a normal childhood. In their landmark study on divorce, Wallerstein, Lewis, and Blakeslee (2000, preface) state, that

> Divorce often leads to a partial or complete collapse in an adult's ability to parent for months and sometimes years after the breakup. Caught up in rebuilding their own lives, mothers and fathers are preoccupied with a thousand and one concerns, which can blind them to the needs of their children.

Such disruption in parents' lives often results in parentification and isolation of children. This is precisely what must be derailed in and after the divorce process. So, after divorce, the task of parents is to allow one of the strongest attachment of their lives to die, and to enhance the secure attachment of their children at the same time. How difficult a task is this!

There is tremendous loss in a divorce. Perhaps the greatest loss is the loss of involvement in the children's lives. This is often something not well thought out in a divorce. It is also something that often turns into a competition for the children's loyalties and affections. Unfortunately, parenting post-divorce is not a competition. But both parties in the divorce, because they have agreed to a divorce, have voluntarily agreed to forfeit some time with their children. (The exception would be in cases of child abuse and termination of parental rights.) Most divorced people do not have this at the forefront of their thinking. When faced with the fact that on Saturday they will not be at the breakfast table with their babies, they are not thinking that this is their choice. It is quite the opposite. Many are thinking about how they can get more time, or somehow change the circumstances so that they have more time, an arrangement that looks more like they have the children every day. This results in competition. Often in the volatile relationship between exes, parents withdraw their involvement to remove themselves from conflict (Emery, 2016) and to get away from the pain of the reality of their loss of time with their children. This has an adverse effect upon a child, who may interpret this withdrawal as rejection. So, we are left with interrupted attachment, and a sense of abandonment in the child. Or we are left with two parents fighting and competing for time, with multiple litigations and thousands of dollars spent.

One might argue that the type of intervention I propose is only necessary for toxic relationships. I would say that every divorce has the potential for toxicity because it is the dissolution of attachment, which is both grievous and potentially toxic. I have found in my work that even the most civil of dissolved marriages are fraught with hurt. This hurt is precisely what seems to motivate parents to fight over custody and to unwittingly create conflicts of loyalty and alignment in their children.

So, co-parenting is a necessary journey, which divorced parents must navigate together after divorce. What is co-parenting? The mid-1990s marked the beginning of the co-parenting movement (McHale, Kuersten, & Lauretti, 1996). This was focused on two-parent families initiating two-house living and parenting. Co-parenting in the twenty-first century can be defined in a broader sense as parenting cooperatively with others. These "others" may be ex-spouses, grandparents, or significant people in a child's life. In my practice I have worked with grandparents who have joint custody of children whose parents are deceased, and the issues are much the same as issues faced with the traditional two-parent divorced family. Elements of loss, competition, and insecure attachment are all present. McHale and Lindahl (2011, p. 4) state that "This basic notion—that children are part of a family relationship system in which they are simultaneously cared for and socialized by multiple parenting figures—is at the core of modern co-parenting theory and research." In other words, the family system as we have known it historically is changing. More people are involved in the care and raising of children, and co-parenting concepts often apply to all, rather than just to Mom and Dad. McHale and Lindahl state aptly (2011, p. 10):

> Co-parenting alliances can function as resources in all manners of family systems for virtually every child—whether that child is raised by a married heterosexual mother and father or by any and all other honorable sets of individuals who step forward to assume and share the responsibility for the child's care and upbringing.

In my practice I have found that the principles and practices I instill in parents are applicable to any family system struggling to come to a unity of purpose and effectiveness.

So, co-parenting can be defined as a "joint enterprise" (McHale and Lindahl, 2011, p. 16) between adults who have banded together to raise and care for common children. In essence it is a family system where two or more individuals have taken on the job of parenting children, outside of the traditional two-parent, married-couple model, or within the two-parent system, post-divorce. The distinguishing factor of a co-parent is his or her consistent emotional involvement with the child(ren). In this manual the idea of co-parenting is assumed to be post-divorce, and/or when there has been a disruption in the consistent care of children where there has been the loss of one parent, both parents, or a radical change in parenting structure which requires an emotional adjustment outside the norm for the children. This could also include non-marital parenting of children when the parents are not co-habiting.

Why is co-parenting education and training so important? First of all, children who have experienced divorce and radical change are often traumatized by the changes and loss they are experiencing. In *The Unexpected Legacy of Divorce*, Wallerstein, Lewis, and Blakeslee (2000) conclude that the effects of divorce are so far-reaching that the final effects are not even visible until children grow up and have intimate significant relationships as adults. And then, there can be devastating effects. Effective co-parenting can stave off many of the negative effects of divorce by developing a new secure base for the children after the divorce. Most negative effects that children experience are related to insecurity, not belonging anywhere after the divorce, and becoming inappropriately triangulated into the litigious or negative relationship between their mother and father. Parent education which pinpoints the effects of negative behaviors in the parent relationship and which guides parents to develop new skills may well prevent some trauma that has been historically normal for children of divorce.

Some states require parent education after divorce. Oklahoma and Maine are two states that have programs which require divorcing couples to be educated in the effects of divorce on the children and in developing a co-parenting relationship. Maine uses a program called I-COPE, which is an "intensive 9 week course, which utilizes psycho-education and emphasizes changing behaviors" (www.kidsfirstcenter.org/for-parents.html#coparenting). In Maine parents are court-ordered to attend these group sessions together and there have been positive outcomes. In Oklahoma parents who are divorcing are required to take a group class prior to or directly after divorcing (www.tulsaworld.com/home-pagelatest/new-oklahoma-law-requires-class-before-many-divorces/article_be443a5a-db28-5f84-81a4-86186ca20d7e.html). The parents may attend together or separately. California, Utah, Missouri, and many other states require and/or offer classes in co-parenting. Some of these classes are offered online. All of the face-to-face classes are offered as a group.

The program I have outlined is unique because the divorced parents are required to attend together without a group, in my therapy office. I operate from the premise that these people will be required to be "in the same room" for many events in their children's lives after their divorce. I consider it to be practice for parents getting used to being together after divorce. The program is also designed to get the parents some necessary experience in communicating about their children after divorce. Many of the parents I see have not been in the same room communicating for weeks, months, and sometimes years. The program is designed to both educate and challenge the individual parents to develop communication skills and common decency with regard to each other.

Many divorced people come to therapy to work through their own grief and trauma post-divorce. This program is not a substitute for personal processing of loss. Instead it is an opportunity for the divorced couple to be educated about divorce and its effects upon them and their children, and to develop a new pattern of relationship which is de-escalated and which focuses on what is in the child's best interest. It's a transitional tool for parents to move out of grief into action in parenting. It also affords divorced parents a safe place where their parenting concerns can not only be heard (as they would be in individual therapy), but also addressed in the presence of a trained professional. Another benefit is that an ongoing relationship can be developed between the couple and the therapist so that any future stalemates can be addressed with the therapist. This program is yet another support for the divorced and divorcing person. Given the fact that adjustment to divorce is an ongoing process (consensus says that it takes up to two years), another support specifically geared toward the parenting relationship is warranted.

Skillset Required for the Work

Since attachment is the basis of psychological health, it is imperative that co-parenting be seen through an attachment lens and that the skills that enhance attachment be used in this work. But it is tricky business. We are confronted with a couple which has forsaken their quest for a marital bond. Yet they long desperately for a deeper bond with their children, whom they are afraid they are losing (often in high-conflict divorces). So, the challenge becomes: how can we as therapists honor the choice the couple has made to divorce and dissolve their attachment bond? How can we respect this choice, be sensitive to the storm of hurt and hatred that might accompany the choice, and still be empathetic with each member of the parental dyad? How can we as therapists also seek to enhance the deep parental bond each of the parents has with their children, while de-escalating the parents' negative relational pattern?

In her book *Love Sense*, Susan Johnson (2013, p. 195) describes a couple who are escalated and dis-attached:

> As the cycle of hostile criticism and stonewalling occurs more frequently, it becomes ingrained and defines the relationship. These episodes are so aversive and destructive that any positive moments and behaviors that occur are discounted and marginalized. And as a couple's behavior narrows, so do the partners' views of each other. They shrink in each other's eyes; the full panoply of their personalities shrivels down to a few noxious traits. She's a carping bitch; he's a withholding boor. In such a darkening environment, partners question every action or comment the other person makes. Psychologists refer to this as a process of escalating negative appraisal, where every response is seen in the worst possible light. Both partners become hyper-vigilant for any hint of slurs and slights, abandonment and rejection. They cannot give each other the benefit of the doubt even for a minute.

Of course, Johnson is speaking of a couple in marital therapy, where she will work to develop a connection or bond. Some of the couples with whom she works will go on to rediscover their emotional connection. Others will not, and they will be stuck in this negative relational pattern. I believe that this quote very accurately describes a couple who have forsaken the quest for the marital bond, and end up divorced and fighting over their children. I have seen this time and again in my office. This description depicts the challenge we have before us. How can we somehow honor the person's decision to divorce while de-escalating their bitter pattern with their ex or soon-to-be ex? And if attachment in fact is the key to gaining emotional ground, how do we bring attachment into the room without disrespecting the couple's choice to divorce?

I believe that we need to find an attachment which is active for the parents and which they currently cherish. This is necessary for them to be able to re-organize their pattern and shift their focus positively onto rebuilding their lives and the life of the family with its new structure. The most likely attachment to emphasize is their attachment to their children. Both parents are emotionally attached to their children. We can extrapolate that this is a common bond between them as well. And it may very well be the only common bond that the parents hope to recognize at this point. If we can turn the parents' attention to their mutual love for their children and their mutual purpose of rearing them well, we may be somewhat successful in de-escalating the negative relational pattern between the divorcing parents.

In addition, we can use our skills of empathy and reflection to assist in the de-escalation process. In Emotion-Focused Therapy the first step in the de-escalation process is to recognize the negative pattern, which has derailed the bonding process of a couple. In co-parenting we have already recognized the negative pattern, and that is always a variation on a theme. That theme is: "I don't trust you." And in the co-parenting after divorce process, it may be too much to expect to rebuild trust in a couple who are fraught with hurt and unwilling to spend inordinate amounts of time in therapy together after divorce. After all, this is not post-divorce therapy. Our goal is civility, respect, and emotional disconnection between the parents, not the renewal of the broken attachment bond of marriage.

So, the pattern is one of mistrust and hurt. In my experience, even in the best of situations between divorced people, there is always hurt. We are not going to change these things. Therefore, the aim is to get these people used to being in each other's presence again, and to redirect their relationship to that of parenting only, rather than processing rejected romance. This is a huge shift for most divorced people. If we develop a bond with each of the parents through empathetic reflection and listening well (i.e. developing a therapeutic relationship), and if we expect the divorced couple to be "in the room together", the de-escalation process will commence. Often the fear of facing each other and having to talk may be the first hurdle to overcome.

Then we use empathy with each parent and with both parents to move them into thought about their children and how their expressed pain may be affecting their children. All of the therapy is aimed at a focus on the relationship of the children to the parents and their divorce. Indirectly we will work on the actual co-parenting relationship, by enhancing each person's attachment bond to their children. In the end, a strong and emotional attachment bond to a shared child becomes a more respectful stance toward the other parent.

How to Use This Book

This book is intended to be a workbook/training manual. Each chapter will outline an issue, which is also presented in the therapy session. There will be a short discussion of the topic with some helpful hints on how to present the material. A handout with questions for your clients follows the discussion of each topic along with a personal reflection. Then there will be an outline to use if you would like to, to present the material to your clients. Chapter 7, "Developing the Co-Parenting Plan", includes a template for the plan itself. The final chapter deals with the ethical issues and challenges of the work.

1 This Is Not Post-Divorce Therapy

In the first session we set the stage for providing a safe place for the couple to work through their parenting differences and lay a foundation for the development of a workable parenting plan. There should be an emphasis on the fact that they will be parenting together until either they or their children die. In most cases this is over 30 years. In those 30 some years there will be countless family celebrations and gatherings where they will have to be side by side. There will be weddings, graduations, funerals, births, concerts, award ceremonies, and sporting events, not to mention funerals and regular holidays and birthdays. (Many couples opt to celebrate children's birthdays together, at least in the early years after a divorce, if the children are younger.) I usually give the example of a young couple that is in a quandary because they are in love, ready to get married, and afraid to invite their parents for fear of a scene. The couple needs to get a vision for the fact that this co-parenting is a lifelong process and that divorce didn't negate this responsibility. If anything, divorce makes the process of parenting more difficult.

It is important that the therapist realize how challenging this situation may be for the couple. They may have had a contentious divorce, which may have been followed by years of litigation and contention regarding the children. (Often couples are court-ordered to come to me after they have been divorced for years, and litigated intermittently throughout those years.) Particularly in court-ordered situations, both parties may have a long history of negative interactions. These interactions may have been fraught with contention and bitterness. They may be embroiled in litigation presently, fighting for custody of the child/children. They may not have been in the same room since their divorce was finalized. Or they may be in the throes of divorce proceedings and there may be a world of hurt between them. In few cases there may be a history of emotional and/or physical abuse. (If these cases are not corroborated by the court, this fact does not negate a person's personal experience.) In short, this is a really hard thing for them to do. It takes a tremendous amount of courage to come into a therapist's office with an ex-spouse, especially if it is court-ordered.

The first session is an opportunity for the therapist to allay fears and set ground rules so that the couple can actually get to work. It is also a session where the therapist begins to affirm both parents and commend them for the courageous act of coming to co-parenting. It is essential to remember that these clients are uncomfortable and frightened. If they are in litigation they may be very wary of you as a therapist, and they may wonder if what they say might be used against them. They may be frightened that abuse will happen in your therapy room, and that they will not be protected. So, there is a lot to be careful with and sensitive to as a therapist.

First, ground rules for the therapy must be set. The couple needs to be informed of the sequence of the sessions and what will be expected of them. They need to know that there are four psycho-educational sessions aimed at educating them about divorce and its effects upon them and their children. They need to know that they will not be expected to really interact in the first four sessions, and that you will be talking to them and discussion will be limited. This format gives the couple some time and experience to feel the safety of space that you have created. This four-session hiatus on discussion allows the couple to begin to get used to being in the same room without arguing or being threatened. Many couples will ask if they can see you individually first. I have a policy that I will not do this until the psycho-educational sessions are finished. The reason for this is that during the first four sessions they will be taught and challenged to change their stance toward each other, and if they meet with me individually sooner, they will only air their grievances and it will not necessarily be helpful. The first four sessions give a backdrop to their relationship with each other, and often soften parents' attitudes toward one another. These first four sessions provide an example of what it is like to be safe with each other. Discussion is very limited and I maintain control of these sessions to assure emotional safety for all.

It is essential to begin with "informed consent". Confidentiality and neutrality must be discussed. I make a point of saying that I am not on either side, and that I am there for their children, to help them be the best parents they can be considering their situations. The focus of the therapy process is on developing a good and workable co-parenting relationship, which can be sustained for years. It is important that you share any personal history of divorce and co-parenting or that you have working with children of divorce or divorced couples. In any case, it is important to use your own experience and "heart" to win the couple over to the therapeutic process. These people are not coming as "normal" clients do, to hopefully find someone they can trust and who will help them. Instead, they are coming with mistrust and a healthy cynicism about what may or may not happen. Whatever distrust they have for their ex-spouse will be projected in the therapy room. This is not something that needs to be dealt with face on. Rather, be aware and realize that it will hopefully dissipate as we process co-parenting. So, initially, the process should be outlined as a number of psycho-educational sessions (four), individual sessions (one each), and sessions where a practical co-parenting plan is authored by the parental dyad (one to four, depending on the couple), and a family session focused on reconciliation. I emphasize that the first four sessions are designed to include very limited discussion, if any. And I assure them that before we begin the co-parenting plan creation, they will have an individual session where they can share their concerns personally with me. You are giving the couple an overview of what this will look like. This will allay their fears to a certain extent.

The first proclamation in this process is that co-parenting therapy is NOT post-divorce therapy. Express that your expectations are not to make another marriage, but rather to help the couple learn to parent together. These people are being asked by the court, or by their own situations, to do the most difficult task imaginable, parenting, with someone that they have lost love and trust with. What a scary journey! Being in your office may be a definitive act of courage, which speaks volumes as to their love for their children. And this is your focal point: Their love for their children. The therapist focal point is "the benefit of the children". This will be revisited over and over again.

Begin the first session with a genogram or timeline of their relationship. You want a bird's-eye view of the situation in which these people are attempting to parent. This genogram also refers to the shared history of the couple, which will lend insight into the major issues of any brokenness in the co-parenting relationship. You also need to know the outside influences and challenges that will affect/have affected the parenting process. This should include how many years they have been married, previous marriages, how they met, how many children (ages, grades, situations), other children from other marriages, grandparent relationships and how involved they are with the children, any exposure to domestic violence and/or addictions, and who else is involved (relatives, step-parents, and significant others). You will want to know the present custody arrangement. If at all possible, having a copy of the court documents pertaining to divorce and custody will help you to understand the situation. You will also want to ask if they are presently litigating and what outcomes they hope for. Although this is a somewhat sensitive question if couples are in the midst of a current litigation, it is helpful to recognize the elephant in the room, and acknowledge it. At this point I also point out the difference between the role of a lawyer, which is to help them win their case, and my role, which is to help them to come to a conclusion together. I emphasize the importance of their lawyer's protective role in a legal action, and I reiterate that I am not taking sides, and that they will do well to work together. I often point out that if they have litigated more than once, they have spent their child's education. I also point out that litigation takes on a persona of its own, and often makes the animosity between co-parents worse. I warn them to be protected by their counsel without becoming more acrimonious.

It is important to note that as a co-parenting therapist your stance must be neutral. You cannot take sides, although you may be sorely tempted at times. Both members of the parental dyad must feel safe with you. This is a difficult task because often co-parents come to your office because they have been court-ordered or because they want to use you in their particular agenda. It is often a minefield. Also, therapists, as in any type of therapy, have to face their own countertransference issues. Personalities and personal experiences can all contribute to our reactions. It is important to maintain an open stance toward each parent. In the first session I openly ask the couple how they communicate and how they are getting along. Often they tell me that they are not getting along, or that they only communicate by text or phone or e-mail. It should be noted that more often than not, in high-conflict divorce situations, one parent will accuse the other of being a narcissist. The only diagnosis that should be taken seriously and addressed is a diagnosis shared by a psychologist who has evaluated the individuals. Terms like bipolar and narcissist are common by-words used by non-professionals. Releases of information should be obtained to gain insight from the children's therapists, ad litem attorneys, and psychologists and counselors who are familiar with your clients. These may be helpful to assist in developing a supportive perspective toward your clients.

After getting a thorough history, there are several essential points to communicate. These should be covered in the first session after obtaining a history and genogram. First you set the stage by being empathetic with their loss. Educate them that divorce is a great loss. Encourage them to grieve. One cannot parent effectively after divorce until the co-parent has allowed him/herself to grieve over his or her own losses resultant from the divorce. When divorce happens, even if it is a divorce that each parent agrees with and feels is necessary, there are great losses. Parents may lose property and things. They lose the dream that they would make a life with, and grow old with, the partner. They may lose friends who often scatter due to being uncomfortable. They may lose their home. They may lose a friend and lover. But the greatest loss, which is often not addressed, is the loss of their right to see and be with their child every day of their life. When they divorce they willingly give up time with their child, no matter what the custody arrangement is and no matter who has "primary custody". This is the painful truth that they are confronted with in co-parenting therapy. This is where bitterness, anger, fear, and mistrust crop up. It is essential to express to the couple that unless they allow themselves to grieve through their losses, resentment and anger will leak into their parenting and this will be destructive to their children. Divorced people can carry anger and resentment and hurt even if they have moved on to new relationships. It is important to note this and to encourage each parent to seek their own counsel and comfort for these issues. Professional and non-professional help can be therapeutic, as long as the parent has allowed him/herself to grieve. I emphasize that grief is the doorway to moving on from the pain and hurt of divorce to developing a new life.

The second point which is made is that their child/children have only one mother and one father and that is them. I point out that the children may have wonderful role models in aunts and uncles and grandparents and step-parents, but they are the only biological parents that the children have. In cases of adoption I emphasize that they are the parents responsible for the child/children. Because of this, it is important they cultivate a healthy respect for each other in this position. I point out that they cannot parent the child/children alone. They are the most important people in their children's lives, and they are essential to their growth and wellbeing. Their children need them both. And whether or not they like it, they will be parenting these children together for their whole lives. They simply cannot negate the fact that having children ties them inextricably together for the rest of their lives. So, it is essential that they develop the ability to appreciate each other in the parenting role. Dad must respect Mom in all of her "Mom" wisdom. And Mom must respect Dad in all of his "Dad" wisdom. I point to Mom and state that she has Mom wisdom and understanding, and I point to Dad and state that he has Dad wisdom and understanding for the child/children. It is possible that either parent may actually be an insensitive or bad parent. But the fact is that they are a parent to the child/children and they do have some creative voice in the parenting process, no matter how they have failed in the past. I emphasize that this respect for the other is based on the person's position in the child's life, that of mother or father, not on good character or successful choices. In addition, the child needs to recognize this mutual respect for his or her own successful development. The fact is that when most couples seek this therapy they have no respect for each other in any area. It is likely that one or the other has had a track record of earning the opposite of respect from their ex-spouse. Co-parenting therapy will hopefully change this course and assist the parents in separating their own issues with each other from their parenting practices. In this session I introduce the concept of emotional neutrality. After the grieving process it is possible for these people to pull away emotionally and begin to develop mutual respect.

That leads into the next point. Co-parents are charged with responsibility for the safety and security of their children. Divorce disrupts a very basic secure base, which the child has depended upon, perhaps for years. When parents separate and divorce, changing the landscape of the child's home and life, the once known secure base is altered immeasurably. The child's "normal" changes completely. Even if the marriage of the parents was not ideal and the child was exposed to fighting or animosity, that was the child's secure base, the only secure base that the child has known. Separation and divorce shift reality for the child, and for a time, that child is left hanging without a secure base, wondering where he/she belongs and where he/she can rest. Often the child will gravitate toward school, favorite coaches and teachers, friends and their families. All of this is an effort to re-invent security. Especially in an acrimonious divorce, the children are challenged to find security elsewhere. Here we introduce the idea that it is the co-parents' responsibility to provide safety and security for their children and to define what this looks like for them. Figure 1.1 shows a series of three sets of circles. The first set depicts a safe and secure family. Two rings intertwine like a Venn diagram with parents and children depicted. This is what children perceive as safe and secure: Mom and Dad in the home and everyone emotionally attached. This is a picture of the child's secure "normal".

This Is Not Post-Divorce Therapy 7

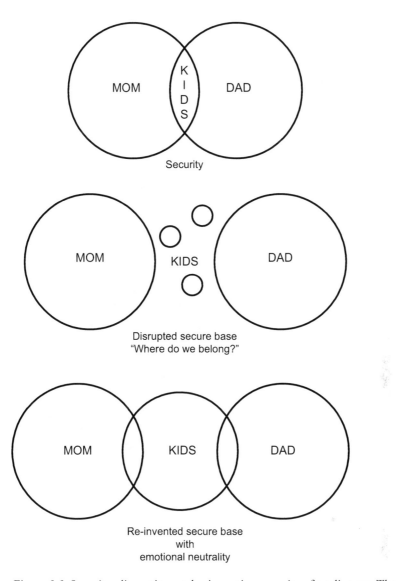

Figure 1.1 Security, disruption and reinventing security after divorce. The progression of co-parenting

The second group of circles depicts what happens when separation and divorce occur. The two circles are apart and the children depicted as small circles floating. The children are looking for a place to land after divorce. They are looking for safety, and Mom and Dad are responsible for that safety. Often both try to provide this in their separate living situations. But if the parents are contentious, if they are prone to speaking ill of one another, they are negating whatever efforts for security they have made for their child. If the child does not sense approval by one parent for the other, he/she is plunged into a battle and forced to "make a choice". This choice might not be outwardly expressed by the parents, but the child senses the discord and does not feel safe in either home. This is a recipe for insecurity and disruption for the child. It is an untenable situation for a person whose life is dependent on outward security and attachment for optimum development. This is also dangerous in a joint custody situation where parents have equal time. Many therapists state that if the children sense animosity in either home, they will not feel comfortable in any home. This leaves the child essentially emotionally homeless. Every custody agreement that I have ever read has stated that the parents are not allowed to speak ill of each other in the presence of the children. This is a pretty common practice among divorced people, particularly at the onset of separation and divorce. It is essential for the parents to understand how damaging this can be for their children.

The third set of circles introduces the goal for co-parenting. Two circles with a circle in the middle are connected with each parent circle without the parent circles intertwining at all. This illustrates our stated goal. We want to develop a new secure base for the child where the parents parent from an emotionally neutral state, providing secure attachment for the children and reinventing the original model of a safe and secure space. In this new model, the parents are emotionally disengaged from each other, yet fully engaged with the children. This is no easy task but it can be developed as the parents disengage from each other, and develop a new relationship based on parenting and love for their children rather than love for each other. David Farber (2013) discusses this as a business relationship or partnership, with the children being the product, and the parents on a development team working together to develop the product. I see it as a fully committed love relationship based on attachment to their children and their common love for their children. If you as a therapist can key into this love and commitment toward the children, you will pave the way for successful co-parenting. Of course, many people are not ready to move away from hatred, anger, and resentment. Hopefully, during the co-parenting educational process they will catch a glimpse of the possibility of moving on. "Think Switzerland" is the motto.

Emotional neutrality entails more than "not loving" the other person. Often parents who come to me are tied at the hip. Many have been litigating for more than two years. They state that they do not love each other. Many have moved on to new relationships through remarriage. They believe that they have accomplished emotional separation because they no longer love each other. This is a fallacy. Co-parents can be emotionally tied for years through negative emotions. These emotions of anger, resentment, and hurt have the same effect as love in their co-parenting relationship, if not stronger. These people remain tied together for years through their anger and hurt and pain. This negative emotion then begins to permeate the co-parenting. And again the child is in the middle. I encourage them to grieve their losses and move forward to respect the other parent as the parent of their child, rather than someone who has inflicted pain, even though that may be the case.

In addition, parents have limited emotion. Understanding the concept of the "emotional bucket" may be helpful in the process. Every person has only so much emotion to hold and express. Pose the question: If you have limited emotion, why would you want to expend it on someone whom you have chosen not to relate to? Would it not be more helpful to expend emotion on people who are energy givers, who give to us and who enhance our lives? Again, negative emotions can tie people together just as strongly as positive emotions. It is not enough to state that you no longer love someone. If hatred and anger are expressed regularly, these emotions can tie the couple together even after they have moved on to other relationships. Our goal is to separate emotionally, to admit the fact of divorce, and to develop emotional neutrality. Emotional neutrality will enable them to focus on their children rather than their own hurt.

Another aspect to introduce is the idea that as the parents provide security for the children, they must allow the children a sense of their own history. During and after divorce, many people want to eradicate their ex-spouse from their lives. Parents must remember that this may leave the child with very little sense of family history. The family history that may be painful for a co-parent may be a source of security and happiness for the child. Parents must be prompted to allow and encourage their children to recall their history with the parents when they were together, if they choose to do so. Also, if this is encouraged it will reinforce the concept that the child was and is a wanted child. If for any reason the child feels like he or she is unwanted as a result of a difficult divorce, this will negate that trend. Children may tend to correlate their own belonging with their parents' belonging. It is essential that co-parents are active in reinforcing the wanted-ness of the children, and the goodness of their family history. It is common for one or the other parent to pull away from the children out of discomfort with their ex-spouse, or with the negative connotations of their relationship. Encouraging a shared history will combat this common practice, which often is hurtful to the children.

After these concepts have been introduced, they must be reviewed. Remember that this is a session where you are casting a vision for the process and challenging the couple to reflect on their position in relation to each other and to their parenting of their children. A series of questions is given to the couple to reflect upon as homework. These may be discussed in the next session or processed individually by the clients.

Personal Reflection

This is a reflection on some common feelings that I have experienced in these co-parenting sessions. I started this work in response to young clients who had been adversely affected by their parents' inability to work together. I was very idealistic, thinking that having the parents in the same room and teaching them would remedy these issues easily. I could not have been more wrong. If I have learned anything in three years it is that the hurt and pain of divorce runs deeper than we can imagine. The single most essential element of this therapy may be encouragement for the parents to allow themselves to process their own grief and pain. Many divorced people never allow themselves this experience. Especially if there has been an affair, the partners, especially the "betrayer", often postpone any real dealing with loss. This lends a stance of defensiveness to the co-parenting relationship, which is never productive. Another revelation has been that when a divorce is signed, the parents are choosing to give up their right to see their child daily. This does not sink in readily and is sometimes the root of constant litigation. In every session where I point this out, both parents are sobered and many exhibit apparent emotion. My first co-parenting sessions were disastrous. I strong-armed the couple, trying desperately to keep the sessions under control. My anxiety may have fueled part of the discomfort in those sessions. I am more confident and comfortable now, and am even more convinced that what I do is essential, and that I can have an influence on the future of these parents and children. If knowledge is power, I am lending some power to these people's lives, and helping them move on.

Homework Reflection Questions

1. What losses have you experienced from your divorce? How have these affected you? How do you portray them to your children?

2. What type of example of emotional health are you to your children? Are you a safe place?

3. Have you put your child in a position where they feel like they have to choose between you and your ex?

4. Do you speak ill of your ex in your home, in your child's presence?

5. What do you want to gain from this course of therapy?

6. What are three practical changes that you would like to see happen as a result of this course of therapy?

Questions 5 and 6 will be discussed at the outset of the second session.

Handout for Session 1

This is not post-divorce therapy. The goal of co-parenting therapy is to help you transition from a position of animosity and hurt to peace and respect. Your children need you both, and they need you to get along. The greatest predictor of emotional health for children after divorce is having parents who get along. You will never get along as a married couple again. But if you transition to a position of parenting together, it is possible for you to work together.

Important points:

1 Your children need you both.

2 You are both the most important people in your child's life.

3 The key to moving on is to allow yourself to grieve through your loss. Even if you are glad to be divorced, you have experienced great loss. Your biggest loss is the loss of time with your child. Face these losses, and process your feelings. If you do not, these negative feelings will leak into your parenting.

4 It's your job to provide emotional safety for your children. The most important element in emotional safety is for your child to feel safe and free to love you and your ex in each house, and to be encouraged to do so.

5 Respect for each other AS PARENTS is essential. Respect can be developed as you become emotionally neutral toward each other: Think Switzerland.

6 Be aware of your emotional bucket and where you are investing this valuable commodity.

Please reflect on the following questions. You will be expected to have answers ready to discuss for questions 5 and 6 in session #2.

© 2018, *Working with Co-Parents*, Mary L. Jeppsen, Routledge

Homework Reflection Questions

1 What losses have you experienced from your divorce? How have these affected you? How do you portray them to your children?

2 What type of example of emotional health are you to your children? Are you a safe place?

3 Have you put your child in a position where they feel like they have to choose between you and your ex?

4 Do you speak ill of your ex in your home, in your child's presence?

5 What do you want to gain from this course of therapy? (Discuss at beginning of Session 2.)

6 What are three practical changes that you would like to see happen as a result of this course of therapy? (Discuss at beginning of Session 2.)

© 2018, *Working with Co-Parents*, Mary L. Jeppsen, Routledge

Outline to Use in Session 1

1. Introduce yourself and what led you to this work.

2. Define co-parenting as a lifelong process. They are stuck with each other.

3. Outline the program: Number of sessions, cost, expectations of their participation.

4. Obtain a history of their family including everyone who is involved with the children. A genogram is helpful.

5. Communicate that their child needs them BOTH.

6. Communicate that they are their child's role models for motherhood and fatherhood. Emphasize their continued need for each other in this role only.

7. Discuss the fact that they must grieve through their losses before they are free to co-parent well.

8. Emphasize that they must provide a secure base for their children.

9. Introduce the transition from a secure family to an insecure place to a business relationship.

10. Define a secure base. (No negative talk etc. re. the other parent.)

11. Define an emotionally neutral stance.

12. Introduce the idea of limited emotion.

13. Elaborate on giving the children a sense of their own history.

© 2018, *Working with Co-Parents*, Mary L. Jeppsen, Routledge

2   It's About the Children Now

Children are affected by divorce. The short-term and long-term ramifications of losing the cohesiveness of one's family, and of experiencing secondhand the negative feelings of each parent during the divorce process, can be devastating and damaging to children of any age. In their landmark longitudinal study, *The Unexpected Legacy of Divorce*, Wallerstein, Lewis, and Blakeslee (2000) point out that often the emotional damage in the children of divorce is not evidenced fully until adulthood where they may have grave difficulty in their own intimate and trusting relationships. That is why it is imperative that therapists who work with co-parents must continually remind these parents of their responsibility to help their children adjust. Every session in co-parenting therapy is designed to refocus the parents on their children, but this second session sets a foundational stage for the work. It is essential that the parents begin to see their own adjustment to divorce as intimately connected with their children's adjustment. In session two we want to review the concepts presented in session one, but with an emphasis on the children and common challenges which children face at different developmental stages after divorce. It is important to note that the child of divorce will continue to manifest difficulty as long as the parents are contentious. In this case time does not heal. If parents are embroiled in an acrimonious relationship, the children will continue in their own destructive thought and action patterns.

Couples in contentious divorces often lose sight of their children's feelings by projecting their own experiences and feelings about their spouse on their children. In this session the parents will be challenged to allow the child to process their own experience of the divorce. Parents will be encouraged to allow the child to react to the divorce in their own developmentally appropriate fashion. This session is all about the children . . . what to expect and how to react.

Emotions continue in a divorce for a long time after the legal battle has been fought (and fought often is the correct term). After the legal proceedings are long over, parents continue to adjust. Hopefully they will be transitioning from extreme emotional investment and enmeshment with their partner to an emotionally neutral state. We encourage them to become a sort of business associate with a common job to do. I often use the analogy of their being on a corporate team where there is a project to complete. One would never expect the team members to have to "love" each other. Rather, they would be expected to respect and appreciate each other within the context of their project alone. The project is the extent of their relationship: planning, building, and completing the project together to produce an excellent result. To take the analogy further, I lead a discussion with the co-parents about appreciating each other's gifts and talents in the raising of their child. This is in essence a review of the first session with a little more depth to it.

Now we begin to give the parents some of the children's perspective. The couple needs to know that unresolved feelings toward one another will not go unnoticed by their children. Children who have been exposed to fighting and contention are deeply affected. Children who are protected from outward contention are affected as well. They are tuned in to their parents, and the most dangerous situation, which is common to divorce, is the situation where the child is put in the middle of the mess. I will point out the couple's specific children, their birth order, and what their tendencies might be in relation to keeping the parents happy. Children first and foremost want to keep the status quo. Often children will become the caretakers of the emotional atmosphere of the family. They will do all that is in their power to keep both of their co-parents happy, often to the detriment of their own happiness and mental health. Parents need to see that often the resilience they see in their children is merely an effort to keep the peace, and cover up the child's real feelings. This session aims at shifting the co-parents' attention to their children.

Consider what a child of divorce is adjusting to. First, his or her major source of security has been blown apart. Their family looks totally different now. As depicted in the previous session's diagram, children are floating between two households, looking for a safe place to land. Often one of the parents has had to take up residence in a new place and this may be very uncomfortable for the child. Many children have a difficult time visiting a parent in a new place, especially if they are able to stay in the family home with the other parent. The child wonders if he or she has a resting place in a new environment.

As mentioned before, the child often will feel a sense of responsibility for the divorce as well as for the emotional wellbeing of his/her parents. That is a huge burden for a small child yet it is a survival necessity for the child to have emotionally healthy parents. Instinctively the child feels a responsibility to keep things on an even keel because he or she naturally seeks secure attachment and emotional safety. I usually point out that children will likely do one of two things. They will be pleasers at both households, keeping both parents happy and pleased. Or they will act out to create an alliance between their parents, which produces security because the parents at least appear as if they are on the same team.

The child's sense of consistency and safety is challenged. His/her basis of attachment, the secure base, is different. And although both Mom and Dad strive to make their home happy and safe, unless the child senses that his/her parents are getting along, neither home is safe. The basis of healthy emotional relationships is safety and security with attachment figures (Bowlby, Miesen, & Munnichs, 1986). In divorce this secure base is threatened and often destroyed. The world is no longer safe for the child of divorce, especially if his/her parents are fighting or not speaking.

Consider some of the other changes that divorce forces a child to deal with. He is now living in two homes with two sets of rules. He may have to change schools or neighborhoods. His time and attention is divided between two households and two needy people. Children are intimately emotionally connected with their parents. They know their parents' moods. They generally do not miss a parent's emotional upset. Sometimes there are new authority figures to adjust to. Boyfriends, girlfriends, step-parents, new extended families . . . Sometimes these new people may be who the child perceives have broken the marriage. These, in addition to organizational challenges like moving backpacks, clothing, and security items, may well produce extreme anxiety and/or anger in a child.

When parents do not present a peaceful front to their children, and when they have not processed their own emotions, when there is strife between the ex-spouses, the child is left to "stuff" his own feelings or put his own processing on hold. No matter what, every child will gravitate toward maintaining homeostasis in the family. The child will be forced to "take sides", to protect one of the parents, to "do something" to change the situation. Children's reactions may vary between extreme pleasing to intense acting out. In either case the child is trying to say something. The child is saying that he/she wants normality and peace. Sometimes in an effort to help the child process, parents will allow them to be privy to details about the divorce, and to the parents' feelings. Children become "parentified" and eventually precious moments of childhood are lost. All of this must be communicated to the divorced couple. Oftentimes this is unintentional. Note that divorce can be painful and parents are often swept into the intensity of their own emotion and pain.

It is important to note that most children do not see things in terms of separation and divorce and marriage. All they know is that their protectors are no longer where they were, that their protectors have changed, and they may become fearful and develop a deep sense of abandonment. Communicate to your clients that their children do not see their ex-spouse as they do. And their children have a right to have their own opinion of their parent. Divorce should never be a set up for competition between parents, though it often is. It is imperative that parents make a habit of reassuring their children that Mom and Dad are working together, and that they both love them.

A typical reaction for a child is to internalize blame for the divorce, particularly if the child may have some behavioral problems or if the child is a perfectionist. Communicate to your clients that they need to develop a divorce narrative together to share with their children. People are storytelling creatures (Brown, 2015a). We use story to alleviate our anxiety and stress. When confronted with an unknown our brains seek a story to alleviate the stress of that unknown. We make up a story. This process is instantaneous and in children may appear as a falsehood. But it is really just a coping mechanism to deal with stress and change. Since we need a beginning, middle, and end to our scenarios, we need to provide this for children. If the couple does not, the child will develop his/her own narrative which may not be productive, helpful, or true. If parents do not provide a simple story for their children to hold onto, the children will hold close their own explanation. Remember that children are trying to make sense of this trauma which has just happened. They need to wrap their developing brains around this radical life change. It is the parent's responsibility to help.

It is also important that the children are allowed to keep their own history. In divorce ex-spouses often want to erase the images of their ex-partner. The topic of the ex-spouse is avoided. Often children are not allowed to speak of their Mom or Dad in the respective homes.

Clients need to consider the effect upon the children. What parents are doing when they avoid stories about their ex-partner is denying their children a sense of their own history. This may produce an atmosphere of shame. Brené Brown (2014, 2015a) speaks of the conditions for shame and these are secrecy, silence, and judgment. Hiding reminders of the ex-husband or ex-wife is keeping a secret, judging the worth of a person, and keeping silent memories of that person. Parents do not have a right to deny their children their own sense of history. Every child needs to know their birth story, their early life experiences, and their special memories. Often after divorce, these historical events are not revisited because the parents have developed hate for each other (especially in contentious divorces). Parents need to be encouraged to allow the child to revisit his/her history, and to reinforce to the child that he/she was wanted and loved. Parents must be reminded that it is time for them to transition from their own emotional chaos to sensitivity to their child's emotional needs. Children dealing with the intense changes of divorce will not be well served if they are also dealing with the shame of loving each of their parents in secret.

The next step is to introduce the parents to an outline of children's reactions to divorce in a developmental timeline. I explain each developmental reaction and relate that if a child is not allowed to work through their own emotions and if the divorce continues to be an issue with the parents (through litigation and contention), the child may well get stuck in any of these behaviors and reactions. I use the metaphor of a neon sign which intermittently flashes "DIVORCE" every time the child is exposed to their parent's disagreement and dislike.

Developmental reactions are as follows:

Infants: Anxiety is often transmitted from parent to child. Infants can become fussy and unsettled, particularly if their parents are anxious and upset. Note that this is the age where children develop their attachment style. They need their routine and they need their needs met. Infants also need the opportunity to bond with both of their parents. Obviously, an infant likely has a greater need for Mom, especially if that child is nursing. But bonding with Dad cannot be downplayed as the foundation of the child's attachment is being built. It is important that the father be encouraged to play as active a role as he would like to at this stage.

Ages 2–3: Toddlers may regress in their toilet training, transitioning from bottles to cups, sleeping in their own space, and any other move toward independence. They may need their security items more. They may be clingy and generally fussy. Note that this is an age where they are continuing to develop their worldview. At age two and three the child is beginning to venture forth away from their primary caregiver, and come back. The idea that they can move away and that Mom and Dad are still there is being developed at this stage. Therefore, the parents need to understand that their presence is important. The child is developing his/her view of the world. Is it safe? Is it predictable? Parents need to do whatever they can for their toddlers to feel safe and secure. During and after divorce this is a major consideration for this age group. Security means seeing both parents, and knowing that they are accessible to the child.

Ages 4–5: Separation anxiety is a possibility at this age. The child is aware of changes and will often miss one or the other parent. The child may cling at exchange times or have a tantrum when having to leave either caregiver. The child may develop anxiety about their absent caregiver and ask lots of questions about their wellbeing. They may develop nightmares or night terrors. They may refuse to go to daycare or school. Separation anxiety is a real condition and it is not something elicited by either parent. Some children have this extreme reaction when being forced to go between parents. Parents must consider that a child this young has no ability to interpret life in terms of separation and divorce, and the fact that his secure base has been disrupted. Separation anxiety symptoms may be interpreted by one or the other parent as the child not wanting to be with the other parent. They may also think that somehow the child has been mistreated in the other household. It is important to note that this is understood as a developmentally appropriate reaction to the upheaval of divorce.

Ages 5–6: At this age the child may manifest some anger and fighting. Anger may be internalized or externalized. The child may act out or, conversely, the child may act like an "angel", while stuffing his/her own emotions. A child at this age may also engage in "I wish" fantasies. The child may say that he/she wishes that Mom and Dad were back together, that they live in the same house, that they have what they had before. These "I wish" fantasies are natural. For a child, it is unnatural to have his parents apart. Children of divorce often will state that they want the other parent to "come home", or that they want both families to live together under the same roof (in a step-family situation). This is natural. Remember that the child is trying to make sense of the changes that have occurred in his life. "I wish" fantasies do not end at this developmental stage. I have had 13-year-olds express a desire to see the parents reunited, even after both parents have moved on to new marriages. The key for co-parents is to know that this is natural, and that their response should be a simple empathetic statement such as, "I know, it's hard that we are not together anymore. I understand how you feel." Parents need to be warned not to bring their own emotion into a response. This is about comforting the child.

Ages 7–8: This age is much like the previous stage. The child continues to try to make sense of the changes in his life. The child will likely engage in "I wish" fantasies here as well. The child may also become very sad and express that he misses the other parent. This is an age where the child can get lost in the emotional turmoil of the family. He/she is finally pretty physically self-sufficient. The child is dressing themselves, and able to entertain themselves. This is an age where the child is branching out on their own more than before. It would be very easy for parents to forget that the child has a deep emotional need for the parents' presence and influence. It is important that divorced parents develop empathy for the feelings of a child this age, so that the child feels safe in expressing his/her feelings. It is important to note that children this age are watching their parents intently. Hearing any negative and critical talk about either parent will damage the child's security with both parents.

Ages 9–10: Psychosomatic complaints may become prevalent at this age. The child's feelings may manifest as stomachaches, headaches, or feeling sick. Remember that many children do not have an extensive feeling vocabulary and may not express what they are feeling verbally. So, their feelings may manifest in their bodies. At this age, children are beginning to understand the concept of divorce and separation. Also, this is an age where the child sees things in a pretty black and white fashion. Hearing anything negative can be very damaging for a child this age, who may be easily swayed to make a choice between his/her parents. No child should ever be asked to make a choice between their parents. Children may also verbalize confusion or embarrassment about the divorce. Depending upon their peer group, they may feel estranged because of having divorced parents. Parents should be encouraged to normalize the situation as they see fit, pointing out other children and parents who are in the same situation. Often children are unaware of their peers being children with divorced parents. Children may also state that they "want to go home" to the other parent during visitation times. It cannot be assumed that the child has been coached to say these things. This is merely a developmentally appropriate response to the child's life changes. Parents need to remember that the child is continuing to make sense of the changes in their life.

Ages 11–12: At this age intense anger and rage may develop. This may be acted out or repressed. In either case, the parent needs to listen to the child's emotional cues. This is an age of transition for all children. It is the onset of puberty. School becomes more demanding. Peers are more influential. A divorce may exacerbate normally negative feelings. If the child's feelings are not recognized or understood, it is very possible that he will distance himself from the parents and withdraw emotionally. This is the age where parents, divorced or not, are setting the stage for their relationship with their child when he/she becomes a teenager. Parents need to be taught about becoming emotionally available to their child, to develop active listening skills and the ability to respond rather than react to the child. An open interchange with a child is not a given, particularly if the child is hurting and confused after a divorce. Parents must take responsibility to listen to feelings, understand and acknowledge hurt, and be available to their children at this age. Parents must step out of their own emotional angst and allow the child leeway to have his own questions and issues. At this stage, parents do not want to develop a pattern of emotional withdrawal in their children. If a child learns that emotional withdrawal keeps him emotionally safe because Mom or Dad is reacting with strong emotion to his/her issues, he/she may develop a negative relational pattern of withdrawal which may hinder intimacy in later life. Parents must be sensitive to their child's emotional expression, allowing the child to experience his/her own feelings without reprisal.

Ages 12 and up: Older children are easily drawn into parental conflict. Parents should never underestimate the ability of their children to know what is going on, to be sensitive to the parents' emotional state. So, it is extremely important for the parents to keep their own feelings of hurt and pain out of the child's awareness. When older children know that there is a disagreement, when they are exposed to arguing, they are immediately forced into making a choice. Who is right? Who is wrong? They may be forced into a conflict of loyalty if they are not protected from this. Taking sides may result in guilt, shame, and repression. It is all too natural for a teen to choose one parent over the other for whatever reason. Older children are often pressured inadvertently and intentionally by parents to choose sides. A common practice of divorced parents is to ask a child who they want to live with. Often parents will tell the child that they can "tell the judge" where they want to live. First of all, most judges will not include any child in a divorce settlement hearing. Second, it is very unlikely that any child, even a teen, can be trusted to be totally honest about his/her wishes to either parent. Deciding between two parents is too emotionally complex for a child. And this choosing will likely become a source of separation and shame. It is my personal opinion that no child should be asked where they would want to live, at least by their parents. This is too emotionally charged. If it is necessary to obtain a child's opinion, the child should be asked by a third party such as an ad litem attorney or a therapist, and the child's opinion should be kept as confidential as possible, to protect them from the guilt of betrayal. The child may also become adept at playing one parent against the other if he/she is drawn into conflict. This is an unhealthy relational pattern. Another reaction of a child this age may be to deny their own emotional struggles and seek to please the parents. In this case, children may learn to develop a pattern of emotional self-denial and people pleasing. This is another unhealthy relational pattern that will affect their adult relationships and patterns of attachment and intimacy.

The second session should help the parents begin to realize how important it is to understand what their children are going through, and how to give them emotional space to work through their own issues pertaining to the divorce. They will learn that they are their children's emotional role models, and that their job is to protect and come alongside their child as they process the ramifications of divorce.

Personal Reflection

Recently I was called into court to help with a four-year-old case where Mom and Dad had been fighting and litigating over the children. Accusations had been made. Compromises had been reached. Compromises had been disregarded. Tempers had flared. And the children are the collateral damage. On this particular day I was asked to vouch for Mom, to say that she deserves compulsory visitation with her teenaged daughter. Mom and teen have a long history of unhealthy relating. Dad is doing his best to "protect" his daughter. The result is a child who refuses to see Mom, and a little brother caught in the crosshairs. One reason for being in Family Court is that Mom wants to change visitation with the younger brother. Both Mom and Dad have strong opinions. Mom says that the child has asked for the visitation to change. Dad states that the child has asked that visitation stay the same. It is a typical scenario. After meeting

(continued)

(continued)

with both parents and their lawyers, the ad litem attorney and I ask to see the boy. He is a preteen. Adorable. Dressed in khakis and a button shirt with his hair slicked back perfectly. He climbs into the big chair in the jury room. The ad litem and I are the only others in the room. This is my first time meeting this child. The parents have been my clients and I have met with big sister once. So, I introduce myself and we make some small talk. What grade is he in, his favorite sport? We commiserate on the uncomfortableness of divorce and how hard it is. Then the attorney and I begin to ask about his feelings about visitation. It becomes obvious to us that both Mom and Dad have shared their thoughts with the child. When asked if he would like changes his first comment is that he wants to see both parents without big gaps between visits. He obviously loves his Mommy and Daddy. I then ask him: "If you could have the arrangement any way that you would like it, what is best for you, what would you like? He hesitated. And then he very clearly stated, "I want whatever will make my Mom and Dad happy". At that point the ad litem and I are fighting tears. We have given the child carte blanche, and he thinks nothing of himself, of hauling his backpacks back and forth, of adjusting to two houses every other day, of leaving his neighborhood friends in one place to go to the other on opposite weekends. Instead, he says that he wants to make his parents happy. Previously he has stated to his attorney that he lays awake at night worrying about his parents. At 11 he feels responsible for the happiness of two adults. This is all too typical of children who have parents who choose not to work together for their children. It is a prime example of why co-parenting training is so essential, and why parents must know the consequences of their emotional dysregulation on their children.

Handout for Session 2

Divorce is shocking and painful for your child. It is your responsibility to help your child process the changes he/she is being asked to adjust to. Below is a brief summary of some of the developmental reactions that children have to divorce.

Infants: Anxiety is often transmitted from parent to child. Infants can become fussy and unsettled, particularly if their parents are anxious and upset. Note that this is the age where children develop their attachment style. They need their routine and their needs met.

Ages 2–3: Toddlers may regress in their toilet training, transitioning to bottles, cups. They may need their security items more. They may be clingy and generally fussy. Note that this is an age where they are continuing to develop their worldview. Is it safe? Is it predictable? Parents need to do whatever they can for their toddlers to feel safe and secure. This includes seeing both parents.

Ages 4–5: Acute separation anxiety may develop at this age. The child is aware of changes and will often miss one or the other parent. Symptoms of separation anxiety may include extreme reactions to leaving their primary attachment figure, and/or inappropriate anxiety when separating from caregivers. The child may express worry about one or the other caregiver. They may develop nightmares, and refuse to go to school. Separation anxiety symptoms may be interpreted by one or the other parent as the child not wanting to be with the other parent. It is important to note that this is understood as a developmentally appropriate reaction to the upheaval of divorce.

Ages 5–6: At this age the child may manifest some anger and fighting. He/she may also engage in "I wish" fantasies. These "I wish" fantasies are natural. For a child, it is unnatural to have his parents apart. Children of divorce often will state that they want the other parent to "come home", or that they want both families to live together under the same roof (in a step-family situation). This is natural. Remember that the child is trying to make sense of the changes that have occurred in his life.

Ages 7–8: At this age the child may become very sad and express that he misses the other parent. It is important that divorced parents develop empathy for these feelings, so that the child feels safe in expressing his/her feelings.

Ages 9–10: Psychosomatic complaints may become prevalent at this age. The child's feelings may manifest as stomach aches, headaches, or

© 2018, *Working with Co-Parents*, Mary L. Jeppsen, Routledge

feeling sick. Remember that many children do not have extensive feeling vocabularies and may not express what they are feeling verbally. At this age, children are beginning to understand the concept of divorce and separation. They may also verbalize confusion or embarrassment about the divorce. And they may state that they "want to go home" to the other parent during visitation times. It cannot be assumed that the child has been coached to say these things. This is merely a developmentally appropriate response to the child's life changes.

Ages 11–12: At this age intense anger and rage may develop. This may be acted out or repressed. In either case, the parent needs to listen to the child's emotional cues. This is an age of transition for all children. It is the onset of puberty. School becomes more demanding. Peers are more influential. A divorce may exacerbate normally negative feelings. If the child's feelings are not recognized or understood, it is very possible that he will distance himself from the parents and withdraw emotionally. I tell my clients that this is the age where they will set the stage for their relationship with their teen, and that they need to be emotionally available to their child. If a child emotionally withdraws, this withdrawal reaction may impact future emotional attachments. Be sensitive to and allow emotional expression.

Ages 12 and up: Older children are easily drawn into parental conflict. And they may be forced into a conflict of loyalty if they are not protected from this. Taking sides may result in guilt, shame, and repression. It is all too natural for a teen to choose one parent over the other for whatever reason. In a divorce situation this choosing becomes a source of separation and shame. The child may also become adept at playing one parent against the other if he/she is drawn into conflict. Of course, this is unhealthy. Another reaction may be to deny their own emotional struggles and seek to please the parents. These "pleasers" may develop a pattern of emotional self-denial for their lifetime.

Below are a group of questions for you to consider and answer as you consider your child's reactions to your divorce and his/her new lifestyle:

© 2018, *Working with Co-Parents*, Mary L. Jeppsen, Routledge

Homework Reflection Questions

1. What patterns of emotion and behavior do you see in each of your children as they have adjusted and are adjusting to your divorce (anger, agitation, "pleasing")?

2. What responses in your children seem to be directly related to what they have seen and experienced as your emotional responses to divorce?

2. What changes do you need to make in responding to your children's adjustments to the divorce (listen more, patience, empathy)?

3. What changes do you need to make in relation to your responses to your ex-spouse to free your child to make his/her own emotional adjustments?

Outline to Use in Session 2

1 Review questions number 5 and 6 from the last session: What do you want to gain from this course of therapy? List three practical changes that you would like to see happen as a result of this course of therapy.

2 Set the context for sharing about the effects of divorce on children, explaining the changes that the child must adjust to, and reviewing the need for a child to feel safe and secure.

3 Communicate the child's sense of responsibility for the divorce and for maintaining the status quo of the family.

4 Define parentification.

5 Express how important it is for the parents to communicate their divorce story to the child, so that the child is protected from developing his own narrative.

6 Review the idea of allowing and encouraging the child to have his history and not deny it because of the divorce.

7 Introduce the idea that the child will continue to adjust to the divorce as long as the parents have not. The child will not move on unless they sense that the parents are moving on.

8 Go over developmental reactions to divorce: Infants; Ages 2–3; Ages 4–5; Ages 5–6; Ages 7–8; Ages 9–10; Ages 11–12; Ages 12 and up.

Developmental reactions are as follows:

9 **Infants:** Anxiety is often transmitted from parent to child. Infants can become fussy and unsettled, particularly if their parents are anxious and upset. Note that this is the age where children develop their attachment style. They need their routine and they need their needs met. Infants also need the opportunity to bond with both of their parents. Obviously, an infant likely has a greater need for Mom, especially if that child is nursing. But bonding with Dad cannot be downplayed as the foundation of the child's attachment is being built. It is important that the father be encouraged to play as active a role as he would like to at this stage.

© 2018, *Working with Co-Parents*, Mary L. Jeppsen, Routledge

10 **Ages 2–3:** Toddlers may regress in their toilet training, transitioning from bottles to cups, sleeping in their own space, and any other move toward independence. They may need their security items more. They may be clingy and generally fussy. Note that this is an age where they are continuing to develop their worldview. At age two and three the child is beginning to venture forth away from their primary caregiver, and come back. The idea that they can move away and that Mom and Dad are still there is being developed at this stage. Therefore, the parents need to understand that their presence is important. The child is developing his/her view of the world. Is it safe? Is it predictable? Parents need to do whatever they can for their toddlers to feel safe and secure. During and after divorce, this is a major consideration for this age group. Security means seeing both parents, and knowing that they are accessible to the child.

11 **Ages 4–5:** Separation anxiety is a possibility at this age. The child is aware of changes and will often miss one or the other parent. The child may cling at exchange times or have a tantrum when having to leave either caregiver. The child may develop anxiety about their absent caregiver and ask lots of questions about their wellbeing. They may develop nightmares or night terrors. They may refuse to go to daycare or school. Separation anxiety is a real condition and it is not something elicited by either parent. Some children have this extreme reaction when being forced to go between parents. Parents must consider that a child this young has no ability to interpret life in terms of separation and divorce, and the fact that his secure base has been disrupted. Separation anxiety symptoms may be interpreted by one or the other parent that the child is not wanting to be with the other parent. They may also think that somehow the child has been mistreated in the other household. It is important to note that this is understood as a developmentally appropriate reaction to the upheaval of divorce.

12 **Ages 5–6:** At this age the child may manifest some anger and fighting. Anger may be internalized or externalized. The child may act out or conversely, the child may act like an "angel", while stuffing his/her own emotions. A child at this age may also engage in "I wish" fantasies. The child may say that he/she wishes that Mom and Dad were back together, that they live in the same house, that they

---

© 2018, *Working with Co-Parents*, Mary L. Jeppsen, Routledge

have what they had before. These "I wish" fantasies are natural. For a child, it is unnatural to have his parents apart. Children of divorce often will state that they want the other parent to "come home", or that they want both families to live together under the same roof (in a step-family situation). This is natural. Remember that the child is trying to make sense of the changes that have occurred in his life. "I wish" fantasies do not end at this developmental stage. I have had 13-year-olds express a desire to see the parents reunited, even after both parents have moved on to new marriages. The key for co-parents is to know that this is natural, and that their response should be a simple empathetic statement such as, "I know, it's hard that we are not together anymore. I understand how you feel." Parents need to be warned not to bring their own emotion into a response. This is about comforting the child.

13 **Ages 7–8:** This age is much like the previous stage. The child continues to try to make sense of the changes in his life. The child will likely engage in "I wish" fantasies here as well. The child may also become very sad and express that he misses the other parent. This is an age where the child can get lost in the emotional turmoil of the family. He/she is finally pretty physically self-sufficient. The child is dressing themselves, and able to entertain themselves. This is an age where the child is branching out on their own more than before. It would be very easy for parents to forget that the child has a deep emotional need for the parents' presence and influence. It is important that divorced parents develop empathy for the feelings of a child this age, so that the child feels safe in expressing his/her feelings. It is important to note that children this age are watching their parents intently. Hearing any negative and critical talk about either parent will damage the child's security with both parents.

14 **Ages 9–10:** Psychosomatic complaints may become prevalent at this age. The child's feelings may manifest as stomachaches, headaches, or feeling sick. Remember that many children do not have an extensive feeling vocabulary and may not express what they are feeling verbally. So, their feelings may manifest in their bodies. At this age, children are beginning to understand the concept of divorce and separation. Also, this is an age where the child sees things in a pretty black and white fashion. Hearing anything negative can be very damaging for a child this age, who may be easily swayed to make

© 2018, *Working with Co-Parents*, Mary L. Jeppsen, Routledge

a choice between his/her parents. No child should ever be asked to make a choice between their parents. Children may also verbalize confusion or embarrassment about the divorce. Depending upon their peer group, they may feel estranged because of having divorced parents. Parents should be encouraged to normalize the situation as they see fit, pointing out other children and parents who are in the same situation. Often children are unaware of their peers being children with divorced parents. Children may also state that they "want to go home" to the other parent during visitation times. It cannot be assumed that the child has been coached to say these things. This is merely a developmentally appropriate response to the child's life changes. Parents need to remember that the child is continuing to make sense of the changes in their life.

15 **Ages 11–12:** At this age intense anger and rage may develop. This may be acted out or repressed. In either case, the parent needs to listen to the child's emotional cues. This is an age of transition for all children. It is the onset of puberty. School becomes more demanding. Peers are more influential. A divorce may exacerbate normally negative feelings. If the child's feelings are not recognized or understood, it is very possible that he will distance himself from the parents and withdraw emotionally. This is the age where parents, divorced or not, are setting the stage for their relationship with their child when he/she becomes a teenager. Parents need to be taught about becoming emotionally available to their child, to develop active listening skills and the ability to respond rather than react to the child. An open interchange with a child is not a given, particularly if the child is hurting and confused after a divorce. Parents must take responsibility to listen to feelings, understand and acknowledge hurt, and be available to their children at this age. Parents must step out of their own emotional angst and allow the child leeway to have his own questions and issues. At this stage, parents do not want to develop a pattern of emotional withdrawal in their children. If a child learns that emotional withdrawal keeps him emotionally safe because Mom or Dad is reacting with strong emotion to his/her issues, he or she may develop a negative relational pattern of withdrawal which may hinder intimacy in later life. Parents must be sensitive to their child's emotional expression, allowing the child to experience his/her own feelings without reprisal.

© 2018, *Working with Co-Parents*, Mary L. Jeppsen, Routledge

16 **Ages 12 and up:** Older children are easily drawn into parental conflict. Parents should never underestimate the ability of their children to know what is going on, to be sensitive to the parent's emotional state. So, it is extremely important for the parents to keep their own feelings of hurt and pain out of the child's awareness. When older children know that there is a disagreement, when they are exposed to arguing, they are immediately forced into making a choice. Who is right? Who is wrong? They may be forced into a conflict of loyalty if they are not protected from this. Taking sides may result in guilt, shame, and repression. It is all too natural for a teen to choose one parent over the other for whatever reason. Older children are often pressured inadvertently and intentionally by parents to choose sides. A common practice of divorced parents is to ask a child who they want to live with. Often parents will tell the child that they can "tell the judge" where they want to live. First of all, most judges will not include any child in a divorce settlement hearing. Second, it is very unlikely that any child, even a teen, can be trusted to be totally honest about his/her wishes to either parent. Deciding between two parents is too emotionally complex for a child. And this choosing will likely become a source of separation and shame. It is my personal opinion that no child should be asked where they would want to live, at least by their parents. This is too emotionally charged. If it is necessary to obtain a child's opinion, the child should be asked by a third party such as an ad litem attorney or a therapist, and the child's opinion should be kept as confidential as possible, to protect the child from the guilt of betrayal. The child may also become adept at playing one parent against the other if he/she is drawn into conflict. This is an unhealthy relational pattern. Another reaction of a child this age may be to deny their own emotional struggles and seek to please the parents. In this case, children may learn to develop a pattern of emotional self-denial and people pleasing. This is another unhealthy relational pattern that will affect their adult relationships and patterns of attachment and intimacy.

17 Finally, emphasize that the theme is keeping their child emotionally safe and focusing on getting along for the sake of their child.

© 2018, *Working with Co-Parents*, Mary L. Jeppsen, Routledge

3   The Games We Play

The title of this chapter really defines the subject matter. Divorce is often a cat-and-mouse game when children are involved and custody is an issue. It is common for divorced parents to develop manipulative actions and reactions, which become habits of relating, and these relational habits have a profound effect upon the children involved. Parents are often unaware of their communication habits. They are often so bound up in their hurt and pain that they cannot see what dysfunctional communication is present. When these patterns become ingrained, it is often very difficult to break their momentum.

In session number three we are continuing our psycho-educational stance. However, the topic may be more offensive to the parents and they may become somewhat reactive to one another. Expect this and hold your psycho-educational ground until you finish presenting the material. I introduce this session by saying that most divorced people have unhelpful patterns of communication prior to the divorce, that these patterns may have led in part to the divorce, and that they likely are continuing into the co-parenting relationship. It's not a surprise that two divorced people communicate in a destructive manner. As a matter of fact, when divorced people come to co-parenting counseling they usually cite a lack of communication as their primary reason for coming. Often it isn't really a communication lack. Rather, it is a communication dysfunction. This session is designed to pinpoint the most common communication dysfunctions for divorced and divorcing couples. At this point parents need to be reminded that they are in this therapy to change themselves and not their former spouses. We have established in the past two sessions how essential it is for the couple to face the fact that they are separated emotionally, and that their focus needs to be on their children. In this session we extrapolate to say that they need to look into their own communication habits and reflect on changes they need to make within themselves. They cannot listen in this session to point the finger at the other person, although this will be a constant temptation. Most couples don't even realize that their communication patterns are as destructive as they are. Remember that these parents are trying their best to navigate their own emotional minefields as they parent with someone who has likely hurt them deeply. It is an extremely difficult task to raise a child with an ex-spouse. It is the therapist's responsibility to remain neutral and informative. By the third session the therapist may have some very real insights about each parent. It is important that these insights be shelved until individual sessions are conducted with the parents.

There is no doubt that most divorced parents have developed negative communication patterns with one another. It is common and just a fact of life. After introducing the session and reminding parents to focus on their own communication problems, I challenge the parents to "eat the chicken and spit out the bones", or to apply what they relate personally to themselves. I also ask them to refrain from accusing the other person because it is no longer their responsibility to aid in their ex-spouse's changes. It is important to emphasize to the parents that they are in this therapy to change themselves and not their former spouses. They can only effect change within themselves.

There are 11 unhelpful patterns of communication. As explained above, these are often a part of the cat-and-mouse blame game which parents engage in. Children can be drawn into each of these if they are privy to the parent's emotional resistance to the other spouse, or if they are intentionally drawn into discussions, which they should really have no part in. Again, we must emphasize that the parents are called on to protect their children emotionally. This means that children are never drawn into parental conflict.

The negative patterns of communication are as follows.

Pain Game

This communication pattern is really a form of punishment. When parents are drawn into this pattern of communication they are making an attempt to control their ex-partner and hurt them within the context of the co-parenting relationship. In this pattern parents attempt to inflict pain and confusion and wreak havoc. When parents engage in this, one or the other parent seems to be unwilling to move on, to let go. One or the other parent is bent on making a point, and having the last word. One reaction of some parents in this category is constant initiation of litigation. This is often designed to bankrupt the other person or punish them financially. Various contempt charges ensue over and over again. These may be valid complaints but litigation is threatening and very expensive. Note that in litigation the emphasis is on a party winning. Lawyers are hired to protect the interests of their clients and in custody and divorce litigation this battle can become destructive to the co-parenting relationship. Parents whom I have worked with have complained that litigation takes on a life of its own and traps the parents into a battle even when there was very little battle to begin with. In divorce no one ever really wins, especially the child.

Another way to inflict pain is through changing schedules at the last minute or being irregular with pick-up and drop-off times and places. After divorce most partners develop their own lives, move on to new relationships, and often have new families, new jobs, and new schedules. Changing schedules can be very difficult for someone who is transitioning to a new lifestyle anyway. Divorced men and women may be transitioning to the workplace for the first time in years after being the primary caretakers of the children. They may be transitioning to developing childcare schedules, and workable schedules for the children's activities. Changing schedules at the last minute and/or constant tardiness is a way of irritating and disrespecting an ex-spouse.

A more radical and insidious way to inflict pain is to use the Department of Human Services (DHS) hotline and make reports on the ex-spouse. If the DHS report is made out of spite and anger, it is normally unfounded. But even if the report is unfounded in the end, the child may be interviewed in school. This is a disruption and it is frightening for a child to be questioned about their parent by a stranger. The family may be interviewed. This disrupts the ex-spouse and potentially his or her new family members. This is also a threat to the person's reputation and may result in loss of job or credibility if it is rumored or publicized. All of this happens and the child is put in the middle, retarding that child's ability and progress to move on from the divorce. Most importantly, this type of thing can call into question the integrity of a parent to the child, even if the report is unfounded. Damage is done—and that damage may be irreparable.

The most common form of inflicting pain is in criticism and argumentativeness at pick-up and drop-off times. Arguing and criticism in the presence of the child always causes some pain and emotional suffering to children, even if they do not show their reactions. In the county where I practice, the standard visitation schedule was changed to minimize parental interaction at pick-up and drop-off times for this very reason. Judges seek to minimize the pain and suffering of the children. So, what is the result for the child? First of all, these types of interactions are a really bad example of relationships to the child. This type of behavior also shows the child that it is acceptable to "punish" those who you have disagreements with. It also shows the child that their parents do not like each other and do not intend to parent them together. Any hope that the child may have of peace between their parents is dashed every time they are exposed to these types of negative interactions.

I Wish

As we discussed previously, it is natural for a child to engage in an "I wish" fantasy. It is developmentally appropriate for the child. And it is natural for a child to want his family back to where it was most comfortable for them. However, when Mom or Dad engages in such a fantasy and exposes their child, it is neither healthy nor helpful. When a parent engages in an "I wish" fantasy they confide in their child that they wish that they could be back together with their ex-spouse. Most parents that we work with do not have this issue, but there are some for whom this has come up. They may "wish" that their ex-spouse never left. They may state that they wish that they were living together as they were before. They may commiserate with the child in their own "I wish" statements. The end result is a child who has become the confidante of their parent, and is now dealing with the parent's feelings of grief and loss. The co-parent who engages in this "I wish" fantasy and refuses to accept the fact of the divorce is damaging their child's ability to accept the divorce and move on.

A child who is exposed to their parent's "I wish" statements is less likely to move on or deal with their own grief over the divorce. In addition, the child may well feel ashamed for wanting to move on and/or guilty for moving on. In this the unrealistic parent is depending on their child to handle adult emotions and to circumvent their own feelings about their parents divorcing. Children should never be expected to carry their adult parents' emotional burdens. This behavior is an example of a parent putting their own emotional struggle on their child to lessen their own load. At this point I encourage the ex-spouses to seek their own counselor, or to go to a clergyman or friend to work through their feelings about the divorce. The therapist must reinforce the importance of the parent making a safe emotional space for their child. Being a confidante for a parent is not a safe space for a child.

I Spy

The name of this game is self-explanatory. This may be one of the most common communication patterns after and during divorce. Children are put in the position of being a go-between and messenger with their divorced parents at best, and in the worst-case scenario the child actually reports clandestinely between the two households. Parents sometimes find it easier to communicate through their children. It is one step of "uncomfortableness" removed for them. It is easier than a face-to-face conversation. The problem is that the children's feelings are not taken into consideration when this happens. It is really important that parents realize that this is not their child's job. It is the parents' job to communicate any and all information between households. This is a job that should never be given to the child, even if the information is innocuous. The child of divorce is looking for a secure base. Security for a child means that they are being cared for. If a parent is curious and asks personal questions of the child, it may produce guilt, a feeling of betrayal toward the parent, or at best, discomfort. The child is not a detective. I tell the parents that if they are curious, they need to ask their ex themselves. Reinforcement of appropriate questions should also be given; for example, questions like: "What did you all do?" "Was it fun?" "How was your time at Mom's/Dad's?"

Disneyland Parent

This pattern may have been in place prior to the divorce. Often in any marriage there is a tough parent and an easier parent. Everyone has a different personality and parenting style. Often in marriage, spouses even each other out. So, in parenting one parent may show more mercy while the other is stricter. This may play out differently after divorce, and be exaggerated, where differing parenting styles collide and the child is put in the middle of a battle for his or her affections. In this case the stricter parent becomes the parent who is the bad guy, and the easier parent becomes the good guy. In custodial situations, where visitation is infrequent for one parent, there may be a tendency for the parent who does not have as much time with the child to make his or her time more fun and less stressful by avoiding structure and discipline. When a parent is a "Disneyland" parent, he/she treats visitation time with the child as fun and avoids discipline and structure. The overall effect is that one parent is perceived as the tough guy and the other is perceived as the fun parent. It is understandable that a parent whose visits with their child are infrequent would not want to be heavy or emphasize discipline. It is equally important that children have consistent standards and parenting in both homes. When the "Disneyland" syndrome becomes the major thrust of parenting, the child will eventually feel insecure at the easier parent's home because of the lack of structure.

Generally parents who fall into this practice are acting out of insecurity and a desire to become their child's friend. They may often avoid their real responsibility as a parent. Note that after divorce there is a huge transition from seeing a child daily and going with the flow of the status quo, to developing a whole new way of maintaining a schedule and relating. A parent who has been a bit less active may be very uncomfortable with the new role, and the new relationship. It may be easier to transition by being a bit looser. This may have to do with the parent's personality as well. In contrast, some parents may face this transition by becoming stricter to feel a better sense of control. When opposite parenting styles are put into the transition, often one becomes the "Disneyland" parent. If this persists, the non-Disneyland parent may become resentful that they are expected to do all the work, while the "Disneyland" parent plays. The child will key into this dynamic and may take advantage of it, or eventually tire of it, hoping for consistent structure in both homes. It must be communicated to the parents that there must be consistency between households and structures that both parents are comfortable with.

Property Rights

When parents are stuck in this pattern, children are seen as property to be negotiated for. These parents often litigate repeatedly. Children are used as pawns and often their feelings are not taken into account. Counselors can be used here as well. Children's counselors are asked to testify as to the "unfit" parent's actions. Although there are parents who could be described as "unfit", most parents in divorce litigation are not unfit. Litigation is used to get back at the spouse, to prove their fault and to punish them. Granted, children often "act out" after divorce. Parents who see this as an opportunity for blame of the other parent are those that are engaging in this "property rights" pattern. The effect on the children can be devastating. Litigation is hard on children. Often they are exposed to some of the issues. They are exposed to the agitation and anxiety of their parents in relation to the litigation. And litigation is another situation where the child's powerlessness is reinforced. The child has not initiated the divorce.

They have no voice in this matter. Further, litigation reinforces the fact that someone else is deciding what to do with them, where they will live, how often and when they will visit. The deciders of these things have descriptors like lawyers and judges. Most children have respect for these terms.

In some cases parents and their lawyers ask children to testify in court. This carries with it a whole set of traumatic experiences plus new anxieties and fears for the child. When children are asked to testify in open court or even in a judge's chambers, they are put in a very frightening and vulnerable position. It is also extremely unfair to ask a child to report negative things about either of their parents. Even in cases of child abuse, advocates, counselors, and ad litem attorneys should be testifying on behalf of these minors. When it is absolutely necessary for a child to testify, every effort should be made for the child to be supported and protected. In New York there is a practice of using a courtroom dog to help children feel more comfortable. But in most cases the testimony of a child is not warranted, and the children should be protected. Again, it needs to be communicated that no one wins in a court case. I try to emphasize to my co-parents that no matter who has "custody", they still must work together. In the end the parents of children must learn to speak to each other, and work together.

Wish Bone

This is a situation centered around the parents arguing in the presence of their children. Typically this happens at exchange times, or over the phone while parents are talking or texting. When this happens, children are forced into a quandary where they must choose between their parents. Children do not see their parents in terms of divorce. They do not perceive their parents in the same way that their parents perceive each other. When parents argue in the presence of their children, they place them in a situation that emotionally coerces them into choosing sides. This is both unnatural and unfair for them. Often children do take sides and choose one parent over another. This is often related to how much negative information they have listened to about the other parent. Their choice may also be related to their personality and position in the family after the divorce. For instance, an oldest child may feel responsible to maintain the status quo or emotional balance of the family. They may take on the role of peacemaker and become the negotiator between the parents. Another child, perhaps the baby who may likely be closest to Mom, may take

Mom's side because they feel that she is their protector. Another child who has a close relationship with one or the other parent will choose that parent. In each scenario, the child is being put in an emotionally awkward position that they may later regret or feel ashamed about.

In a situation like this, parents are inadvertently asking their children to practice a form of emotional self-denial. The children are subconsciously asked to deny a whole part of themselves as they side with one parent over another. This can affect their identity development. If they are constantly in a position where taking sides is encouraged, they will eventually deny those parts of themselves associated with the "rejected" parent. Note that most children have been told for years how they are "like" their parents. When parents force the children to choose between them, they are asking their children to choose what parts of themselves are acceptable and which parts are not acceptable. No parent would intentionally ask a child to deny a part of himself. Explaining this process to the co-parents will hopefully make them more aware of the uncomfortable positions in which they have placed their children as they have argued in their presence.

Set-Up

This is a more intense experience for the child of being put in a position of choosing one parent over another. In this pattern, one parent sets the other up to be the "bad guy". In reality there may have been a "bad guy". There may have been a partner who had an affair, or who had a bad temper, or who worked too much and neglected the family. There are countless reasons for divorce. We are not denying these issues. But we need to make it clear to the parents that this pattern of making their ex-spouse the person to blame, the person who broke up the marriage, the person who has made life difficult . . . is destructive to their child. How can a child argue with such a strong opinion of their parent? It is very difficult for children to discern when a parent is telling them what another parent said or did. The child is again forced to make a choice between their parents. This can condition the child to be a pleaser, where he or she learns that it is unacceptable to one parent to support or love the other parent. So, the child learns to stay under the radar, to do and say what pleases their parent. This child may appear to be incredibly compliant, but he or she is learning a pattern of emotional self-denial. Emotional self-denial will be something that will affect every significant relationship they have in their future. It will retard their ability to be authentic in intimate relationships. Another possibility is that the child will develop emotional isolation from their parents and refuse to please and act out behaviorally. This is another way to deny feelings, to cover them with anger.

This is also where parental alienation can occur. It is important to note that setting up another parent to be the bad guy is not necessarily what is termed parental alienation, but it is the first step in the process. Parental alienation is "a generic term used broadly to refer to a child who has been influenced to reject one parent, in extreme cases brainwashed or indoctrinated by an embittered/malicious other parent" (Kuehnle & Drozd, 2012; Saini, Johnston, Fidler, & Bala, 2012, p. 399). Parental alienation is very difficult to prove and to discern. Often the child is just reacting and has been so influenced that there is no boundary between the offending parent's opinion and the child's. Often a child loses out on years of relationship while this is happening. And the child may actually fear their parent, being afraid to ever relate normally to the parent who has been alienated. It is essential that in telling the co-parents about this, they realize that when a parent alienates a child from the other parent, they are producing in their child a sense of abandonment, of not being loved by their parent. The parents need to know that this is generally destructive to the child, to grow up with a sense of abandonment. Abandonment is not easily overcome. Though producing abandonment may make the offending parent feel like they have won a battle for their child's heart, it really is destructive to the child's sense of safety and attachment. A sense of abandonment for any child is not easily repaired. It will affect every relationship that the child pursues for their entire lifetime. Poisoning a child against their parent is also a way of telling them that they are not of worth to the other parent. It will produce an underlying sense of shame, which is the belief that they are not worthy of love or belonging (Brown, 2015b). This alienation also denies the child the right to have their own opinion about their other parent and silences their voice. Again, no parent sets out to produce a sense of alienation in the child whom they love. But we need to raise their consciousness about the effects of their attitudes and actions upon their children.

Blackmail

When this pattern is used, the parents communicate their displeasure with their ex-spouse by communicating displeasure with their child.

It is a way of retaliating against a spouse and using the child directly. An example would be to punish the child for something done at the other parent's home, rather than speaking with the other parent first. The child becomes the object of the parent's anger when the parent is really angry at their ex-spouse. This is really hard for a child because they are powerless to change what occurs in either home. Often the child has no choice and no voice. Here they are truly being used as pawns in an effort to express anger and resentment to an ex-spouse. There needs to be a consistent set of standards in both homes, with consistent rules and consequences, so that this does not happen.

Cutdown

This happens when the child is exposed to direct putdowns of either parent in either home. This may have a direct negative effect on the child's identity development, as explained above. Studies show that children who are not exposed to negative comments about their parents, even if the parents are not harmonious, adjust more readily and successfully than their peers who are exposed to putdowns (Emery, 2016). Every custody agreement that I have read states that the parents are not allowed to speak negatively about their ex-spouse in the presence of their child. I have yet to meet a couple that has abided by this order on a regular basis. When I introduce this concept I emphasize that the child should not hear anything negative about the other parent, about the other parent's family or friends, or about any attachment figure associated with the other parent. I also express that the child should never see an eye-roll or a phone hang-up, or hear an exasperated sigh. The burden of self-control is placed on the divorced parents to protect their children from negativity related to their parents. Sometimes this means that the parents must set strict boundaries with their own parents and relatives who have sided with them in the divorce. Co-parents need to address this issue with their families and friends to assist their children in adjusting to the new life after divorce.

Party Pooper

When a parent criticizes the activities their ex chooses to participate in with their child, the child is put in a difficult position. Often inadvertently, a parent may have a negative or critical attitude about their ex-spouse. This attitude may permeate many comments made about them. Parents need to be careful that their negative attitudes toward one another do not spill into negative attitudes about the child's activities with that ex-spouse. When the child senses disapproval, he or she may feel that they are not allowed to freely enjoy whatever experience they have had or are having with their other parent. The child may be embarrassed and/or angry because their parent has "rained on their parade". And this may affect their further relationship with their other parent. One very important job of a co-parent is to foster a relationship between their child and their ex-spouse. In the short run this will produce a sense of security and trust in their child. In the long run, it will produce a sense of gratefulness in their child as they grow up and realize that in spite of hurt and pain, their parents decided to assist them in developing a good relationship with both of them. Again, this is a pattern where negative attitude and speaking will affect the child. Parents have a responsibility to encourage their children to have a good relationship with their other parent.

Pay-Off

This pattern happens when gifts, privileges, and promises are used as leverage for the relationship with the children. It can happen with children of any age. This is a lot like being a "Disneyland" parent but is more focused on material leverage used to gain loyalty. Here an insecure parent uses money, gifts, privileges, and promises to obtain the child's love and respect. In situations where there is an income differential (as in many divorce situations), this may also be very threatening to the ex-spouse. In divorce, spouses may be forced back into the workforce and may not have a secure income. And this practice may magnify the differential to the children and put them in a position of choosing the parent who can give them more. This may be very tempting, especially with teenagers.

Practicing pay-off may also give the child a false sense of power. The child may feel that they have power over the parent who does not pay them off, and the child may use the fact that one parent will give them more as a form of controlling the parent who can't. It will also teach the child that they can manipulate their parent to give them "stuff" in exchange for loyalty and even betrayal of the other parent. Obviously, a child who has played into this game will eventually regret their own actions, and they may even blame themselves rather than betraying the parent who has drawn them into it. For a child, there is no easy way to overcome such regret. Parents who co-parent need to know that the end game is not who wins the child's loyalty. Co-parents need to know that they are not in a competition for the child's loyalty and love. It is about how the child grows up secure and happy. The parents need to be encouraged to change their focus. This is not a competition. It is a collaboration and a new lifestyle after divorce.

After these "games" are described, I encourage the parents to evaluate themselves in relation to these unhelpful communication patterns. We will normally have a discussion about which ways they see themselves relating and if they are willing to change their patterns. I try to normalize the fact that most divorced people do use one negative communication habit or another. And I try to communicate that they have a chance to change and develop a constructive relationship of co-parenting, looking to the future.

Personal Reflection

Co-parents betray themselves as they communicate in the therapy room. Often the therapist can see just the way they habitually communicate if they are encouraged to speak to each other in your presence. One pattern that is repeated over and over again in my office is what I call the recurring opinion. It happens when one of the co-parents criticizes a particular incident from the past. Often the same offense is revisited over and over again. The parent who is offended will turn to me and get my attention, then ask for permission to relate a story or incident. Usually I have heard the story previously. Before I have a chance to stop it, I am listening to a tirade against the other spouse, who at this point is trying to interrupt by speaking louder and louder. My response is to ask if I might interrupt. I then point out that this incident happened previous to our counseling and that they have both developed poor communication habits. I might address the idea of forgiveness if the couple is not horribly escalated. In other cases I try to emphasize that neither of them are the same person they were yesterday, let alone what they were at the time of the divorce. I point out differences such as the fact that they may have remarried or had another child or changed jobs. This will sometimes redirect the conversation to something more constructive.

Homework Reflection Questions

1. What pattern of communication do I use more than the others?

2. How am I willing to change this pattern for the sake of my child?

3. What areas do my ex and I disagree upon in parenting and how can we come to a better collaboration?

Handout for Session 3

1. **Pain Games**: When parents are drawn into this pattern of communication they are making an attempt to control their ex-partner and hurt them within the context of the co-parenting relationship. In this pattern parents attempt to inflict pain and confusion and wreak havoc. One reaction of some parents is constant litigation. They might change schedules at the last minute or be irregular for pick-up and drop-off times and places. Changing schedules can be very difficult because a person's schedule is interrupted. A radical way to inflict pain is to use the DHS hotline and make reports on the ex-spouse. If the DHS report is made out of spite and anger, it is normally unfounded. The most common form of inflicting pain is in criticism and argumentativeness at pick-up and drop-off times. This puts the child in a difficult position of having to take sides. This type of behavior also shows the child that it is acceptable to "punish" those who you have disagreements with and also shows the child that their parents do not like each other and do not intend to parent them together.

2. **I Wish**: It is natural for a child to engage in an "I wish" fantasy. It is developmentally appropriate for the child. However, when Mom or Dad engages in such a fantasy and exposes their child, it is neither healthy nor helpful. In this "game" the parent states that he/she wishes the parents were back together again. The end result is a child who has become the confidante of their parent, and is now dealing with the parent's feelings of grief and loss. A child who is exposed to their parents' "I wish" statements is less likely to move on or deal with his/her own grief over the divorce. Children should never be expected to carry their adult parents' emotional burdens.

3. **I Spy**: This happens when one of the parents uses the child to transport information from the ex-spouse's home and life etc. The job of communicating any and all information between households is a job that should never be given to the child. If a parent is curious and asks personal questions of the child, it may produce guilt, a feeling of betrayal toward the parent, and discomfort. The child should never be expected to report to either of their parents. The child is not a detective and neither is the parent.

© 2018, *Working with Co-Parents*, Mary L. Jeppsen, Routledge

4 **Disneyland Parent**: This pattern may have been in place prior to the divorce. When a parent is a "Disneyland" parent, he/she treats visitation time with the child as fun and avoids discipline and structure. The overall effect is that one parent is perceived as the tough guy and the other is perceived as the fun parent. When the "Disneyland" syndrome becomes the major thrust of parenting, the child will eventually feel insecure at the more permissive parent's home because children thrive on consistent limits and structure. If the permissive parent is acting out of insecurity and a desire to become their child's friend, they are avoiding their real responsibility as a parent.

5 **Property Rights**: When parents are "stuck" in this pattern, children are seen as property to be negotiated for. These parents often litigate repeatedly. Children are used as pawns and often their feelings are not taken into account. Litigation is hard on children. Litigation is another situation where the child's powerlessness is reinforced. The child has not initiated the divorce. They have no voice in this matter. Further, litigation reinforces the fact that someone else is deciding what to do with them . . . where they will live, how often and when they will visit. This is frightening and threatening to a child.

6 **Wish Bone**: This situation is similar to "Property Rights" but is centered around the parents arguing in the presence of their children. Typically this happens at exchange times. Children do not see their parents in terms of divorce. They do not perceive their parents like their parents perceive each other. Placing them in a situation that emotionally coerces them into choosing sides is both unnatural and unfair for them. The children are subconsciously asked to deny a whole part of themselves as they side with one parent over another. This can affect their identity development. If they are constantly in a position where taking sides is encouraged, they will eventually deny those parts of themselves associated with the "rejected" parent. When parents force the children to choose between them, they are asking their children to choose what parts of themselves are acceptable and which parts are not.

7 **Set-Up**: This is a more intense experience for the child of being put in a position of choosing one parent over another. In this pattern, one parent sets the other up as the "bad guy". It is important to note that setting up the other parent to be the bad guy is not necessarily

© 2018, *Working with Co-Parents*, Mary L. Jeppsen, Routledge

what is termed parental alienation. But it may be the first step in the process. Parental alienation is "a generic term used broadly to refer to a child who has been influenced to reject one parent, in extreme cases brainwashed or indoctrinated by an embittered/malicious other parent" (Kuehnle & Drozd, 2012; Saini, Johnston, Fidler, & Bala, 2012, p. 398). When a parent alienates a child from the other parent they are producing in their child a sense of abandonment, of not being loved by their parent. A sense of abandonment for any child is not easily repaired. It will affect every relationship that child pursues for their entire lifetime. Poisoning a child against their parent is also a way of telling them that they are not allowed to form their own opinion about their parent and that their voice does not count.

8 **Blackmail**: When this pattern is used, the parents communicate their displeasure with their ex-spouse by communicating displeasure with their child. It is a way of retaliating against a spouse and using the child directly. The child becomes the object of the parent's anger when the parent is really angry at their ex-spouse. This reinforces the need to have a consistent set of standards in both homes, with consistent rules and consequences, so that this does not happen.

9 **Cutdown**: This happens when the child is exposed to direct put-downs of either parent in either home. This may have a direct negative effect on the child's identity development.

10 **Party Pooper**: When a parent criticizes the activities their ex chooses to participate in with their child, the child is put in a difficult position. The child is not allowed to freely enjoy whatever experience they have had with their other parent. The child may be embarrassed and/or angry because their parent has "rained on their parade". Parents have a responsibility to encourage their children to have a good relationship with their other parent.

11 **Pay-Off**: This pattern happens when gifts, privileges, and promises are used as leverage for the relationship with the children. It can happen with children of any age. Here an insecure parent uses money, gifts, privileges, and promises to obtain the child's loyalty. This practice will give the child a false sense of power. It will also teach the child that they can manipulate their parents to give them "stuff" in exchange for loyalty and even betrayal of the other parent.

© 2018, *Working with Co-Parents*, Mary L. Jeppsen, Routledge

Outline to Use in Session 3

1 Begin the session by asking how they are doing and if their communication has improved.

2 Review the highpoints of the first two sessions, focusing on the importance of the child's attachment to both of them and his or her emotional safety.

3 Introduce the idea that they may have habits of communication that may have developed either in the marriage or since the divorce. Explain that in this session they will be confronted with some unhelpful forms of communication. They should look for these habits in themselves, not in their ex.

4 Introduce the idea that these forms of unhelpful communication are hurtful to both them and their children, and many of these patterns are habits that can be recognized and unlearned.

5 **Pain Game:** This communication pattern is really a form of punishment. When parents are drawn into this pattern of communication they are making an attempt to control their ex-partner and hurt them within the context of the co-parenting relationship. In this pattern parents attempt to inflict pain and confusion and wreak havoc. When parents engage in this, one or the other parent seems to be unwilling to move on, to let go. One or the other parent is bent on making a point, and having the last word. One reaction of some parents in this category is constant initiation of litigation. This is often designed to bankrupt the other person or punish them financially. Various contempt charges ensue over and over again. These may be valid complaints but litigation is threatening and very expensive. Note that in litigation the emphasis is on a party winning. Lawyers are hired to protect the interests of their clients and in custody and divorce litigation this battle can become destructive to the co-parenting relationship. Parents whom I have worked with have complained that litigation takes on a life of its own and traps the parents into a battle even when there was very little battle to begin with. In divorce no one really ever wins, especially the child.

© 2018, *Working with Co-Parents*, Mary L. Jeppsen, Routledge

Another way to inflict pain is through changing schedules at the last minute or being irregular for pick-up and drop-off times and places. After divorce most partners develop their own lives, move on to new relationships, and often have new families, new jobs, and new schedules. Changing schedules can be very difficult for someone who is transitioning to a new lifestyle anyway. Divorced men and women may be transitioning to the workplace for the first time in years after being the primary caretakers of the children. They may be transitioning to developing childcare schedules, and workable schedules for the children's activities. Changing schedules at the last minute and/or constant tardiness is a way of irritating and disrespecting an ex-spouse.

A more radical and insidious way to inflict pain is to use the DHS hotline and make reports on the ex-spouse. If the DHS report is made out of spite and anger, it is normally unfounded. But even if the report is unfounded in the end, the child may be interviewed in school. This is a disruption and it is fearful for a child to be questioned about their parent by a stranger. The family may be interviewed. This disrupts the ex-spouse and potentially his or her new family members. This is also a threat to the person's reputation and may result in loss of job or credibility if it is rumored or publicized. All of this happens and the child is put in the middle, retarding that child's ability and progress to move on from the divorce. Most importantly, this type of thing can call into question the integrity of a parent to the child, even if the report is unfounded. Damage is done—and that damage may be irreparable.

The most common form of inflicting pain is in criticism and argumentativeness at pick-up and drop-off times. Arguing and criticism in the presence of the child/children always causes some pain and emotional suffering to children, even if they do not show their reactions. In the county where I practice, the standard visitation schedule was changed to minimize parental interaction at pick-up and drop-off times for this very reason. Judges seek to minimize the pain and suffering of the children. So, what is the result for the child? First of all, these types of interactions are a really bad example of relationships to the child. This type of behavior also shows the child that it is acceptable to "punish" those who you have disagreements with. It also shows the child that his/her parents do not like each other and do not intend to parent him together. Any hope that the child may have of peace between his parents is dashed every time he is exposed to these types of negative interactions.

© 2018, *Working with Co-Parents*, Mary L. Jeppsen, Routledge

6 **I Wish:** As we discussed previously, it is natural for a child to engage in an "I wish" fantasy. It is developmentally appropriate for the child. And it is natural for a child to want his family back to where it was most comfortable for him or her. However, when Mom or Dad engages in such a fantasy and exposes their child, it is neither healthy nor helpful. When a parent engages in an "I wish" fantasy they confide in their child that they wish that they could be back together with their ex-spouse. Most parents that we work with do not have this issue, but there are some for whom this comes up. They may "wish" that their ex-spouse never left. They may state that they wish that they were living together as they were before. They may commiserate with the child in his or her own "I wish" statements. The end result is a child who has become the confidante of their parent, and is now dealing with the parent's feelings of grief and loss. The co-parent who engages in this "I wish" fantasy and refuses to accept the fact of the divorce is damaging their child's ability to accept the divorce and move on. A child who is exposed to their parent's "I wish" statements is less likely to move on or deal with his/her own grief over the divorce. In addition, the child may well feel ashamed for wanting to move on and/or guilty for moving on. In this the unrealistic parent is depending on their child to handle adult emotions and to circumvent their own feelings about their parents divorcing. Children should never be expected to carry their adult parents' emotional burdens. This behavior is an example of a parent putting his or her own emotional struggle on their child to lessen their own load. At this point I encourage the ex-spouses to seek their own counselor, or to go to a clergyman or friend to work through their feelings about the divorce. The therapist must reinforce the importance of the parent making a safe emotional space for their child. Being a confidante for a parent is not a safe space for a child.

7 **I Spy:** The name of this game is self-explanatory. This may be one of the most common communication patterns after and during divorce. Children are put in the position of being a go-between and messenger with their divorced parents at best, and in the worst-case scenario the child actually reports clandestinely between the two households. Parents sometimes find it easier to communicate through their children. It is one step of "uncomfortableness" removed for them. It is easier than a face-to-face conversation. The problem is that the children's feelings are not

© 2018, *Working with Co-Parents*, Mary L. Jeppsen, Routledge

taken into consideration when this happens. It is really important that parents realize that this is not their child's job. It is the parents' job to communicate any and all information between households. This is a job that should never be given to the child, even if the information is innocuous. The child of divorce is looking for a secure base. Security for a child means that he or she is being cared for. If a parent is curious and asks personal questions of the child, it may produce guilt, a feeling of betrayal toward the parent, or at best, discomfort. And the child should never be expected to report to either of their parents about their parents. The child is not a detective. I tell the parents that if they are curious, they need to ask their ex themselves. Reinforcement of appropriate questions should also be given.

8 **Disneyland Parent:** This pattern may have been in place prior to the divorce. Often in any marriage there is a tough parent and an easier parent. Everyone has a different personality and parenting style. Often in marriage, spouses even each other out. So, in parenting one parent may show more mercy while the other is stricter. This may play out differently after divorce, and be exaggerated, where differing parenting styles collide and the child is put in the middle of a battle for his or her affections. In this case the stricter parent becomes the parent who is the bad guy, and the easier parent becomes the good guy. In custodial situations where visitation is infrequent for one parent, there may be a tendency for the parent who does not have as much time with the child to make his or her time more fun, and less stressful by avoiding structure and discipline. When a parent is a "Disneyland" parent, he/she treats visitation time with the child as fun and avoids discipline and structure. The overall effect is that one parent is perceived as the tough guy and the other is perceived as the fun parent. It is understandable that a parent whose visits with their child are infrequent would not want to be heavy or emphasize discipline. It is equally important that children have consistent standards and parenting in both homes. When the "Disneyland" syndrome becomes the major thrust of parenting, the child will eventually feel insecure at the easier parent's home because of the lack of structure. Generally parents who fall into this practice are acting out of insecurity and a desire to become their child's friend. They may often avoid their real responsibility as a parent. Note that after divorce there is a huge

---

© 2018, *Working with Co-Parents*, Mary L. Jeppsen, Routledge

transition from seeing a child daily and going with the flow of the status quo, to developing a whole new way of maintaining a schedule and relating. A parent who has been a bit less active as a parent may be very uncomfortable with the new role, and the new relationship. It may be easier to transition by being a bit looser. This may have to do with the parent's personality as well. In contrast, some parents may face this transition by becoming stricter to feel a better sense of control. When opposite parenting styles are put into the transition, often one becomes the "Disneyland" parent. If this persists, the non-Disneyland parent may become resentful that they are expected to do all the work, while the "Disneyland" parent plays. The child will key into this dynamic and may take advantage of it, or eventually tire of it, hoping for consistent structure in both homes. It must be communicated to the parents that there must be consistency between households and structure that both parents are comfortable with.

9 **Property Rights:** When parents are stuck in this pattern, children are seen as property to be negotiated for. These parents often litigate repeatedly. Children are used as pawns and often their feelings are not taken into account. Counselors can be used here as well. Children's counselors are asked to testify as to the "unfit" parent's actions. Although there are parents who could be described as "unfit", most parents in divorce litigation are not unfit. Litigation is used to get back at the spouse, to prove their fault and to punish them. Granted, children often "act out" after divorce. Parents who see this as an opportunity for blame of the other parent are those that are engaging in this "property rights" pattern. The effect on the children can be devastating. Litigation is hard on children. Often they are exposed to some of the issues. They are exposed to the agitation and anxiety of their parents in relation to the litigation. And litigation is another situation where the child's powerlessness is reinforced. The child has not initiated the divorce. They have no voice in this matter. Further litigation reinforces that fact that someone else is deciding what to do with them, where they will live, how often and when they will visit. The deciders of these things have descriptors like lawyers and judges. Most children have respect for these terms. In some cases parents and their lawyers ask children to testify in court. This carries with it a whole set of traumatic experiences for the child. When

© 2018, *Working with Co-Parents*, Mary L. Jeppsen, Routledge

children are asked to testify in open court or even in a judge's chambers, they are put in a very frightening and vulnerable position. It is also extremely unfair to ask a child to report negative things about either of their parents. Even in cases of child abuse, advocates, counselors, and ad litem attorneys should be testifying on behalf of these minors. When it is absolutely necessary for a child to testify, every effort should be made for the child to be supported and protected. In New York there is a practice of using a courtroom dog to help children feel more comfortable. But in most cases the testimony of a child is not warranted, and the children should be protected. Again, it needs to be communicated that no one wins in a court case. I try to emphasize to my co-parents that no matter who has "custody", they still must work together. In the end the parents of children must learn to speak to each other, and work together.

10 **Wish Bone:** This is a situation centered around the parents arguing in the presence of their children. Typically this happens at exchange times, or over the phone while parents are talking or texting. When this happens something interesting happens to the children. Emotionally they are forced into a quandary where they must choose between their parents. Children do not see their parents in terms of divorce. They do not perceive their parents in the same way that their parents perceive each other. When parents argue in the presence of their children they place them in a situation that emotionally coerces them into choosing sides. This is both unnatural and unfair for them. Often children do take sides and choose one parent over another. This is often related to how much negative information they have listened to about the other parent. Their choice may also be related to their personality and position in the family after the divorce. For instance, an oldest child may feel responsible to maintain the status quo or emotional balance of the family. They may take on the role of peacemaker and become the negotiator between the parents. Another child, perhaps the baby who may likely be closest to Mom, may take Mom's side because they feel that she is their protector. Another child who has a close relationship with one or the other parent will choose that parent. In each scenario, the child is being put in an emotionally awkward position that he may later regret or feel ashamed about.

© 2018, *Working with Co-Parents*, Mary L. Jeppsen, Routledge

In a situation like this, parents are inadvertently asking their children to practice a form of emotional self-denial. The children are subconsciously asked to deny a whole part of themselves as they side with one parent over another. This can affect their identity development. If they are constantly in a position where taking sides is encouraged, they will eventually deny those parts of themselves associated with the "rejected" parent. Note that most children have been told for years how they are "like" their parents. When parents force the children to choose between them, they are asking their children to choose what parts of themselves are acceptable and which parts are not. No parent would intentionally ask a child to deny a part of himself. Explaining this process to the co-parents will hopefully make them more aware of the uncomfortable positions in which they have placed their children as they have argued in their presence.

11 **Set-Up:** This is a more intense experience for the child of being put in a position of choosing one parent over another. In this pattern, one parent sets the other up to be "bad guy". In reality there may have been a "bad guy". There may have been a partner who had an affair, or who had a bad temper, or who worked too much and neglected the family. There are countless reasons for divorce. We are not denying these issues. But we need to make it clear to the parents that this pattern of making their ex-spouse the person to blame, the person who broke up the marriage, the person who has made life difficult. . . is destructive to their child. How can a child argue with such a strong opinion of their parent? It is very difficult for children to discern when a parent is telling them what another parent said or did. The child is again forced to make a choice between their parents. This can condition the child to be a pleaser, where he or she learns that it is unacceptable to one parent for the child to support or love the other parent. So, the child learns to stay under the radar, to do and say what pleases their parent. This child may appear to be incredibly compliant, but he or she is learning a pattern of emotional self-denial. Emotional self-denial will be something that will affect every significant relationship they have in their future. It will retard their ability to be authentic in intimate relationships. Another possibility is that the child will develop emotional isolation from their parents and refuse to please and act out behaviorally. This is another way to deny feelings, to cover them with anger.

© 2018, *Working with Co-Parents*, Mary L. Jeppsen, Routledge

This is also where parental alienation can occur. It is important to note that setting up another parent to be the bad guy is not necessarily what is termed parental alienation, but it is the first step in the process. Parental alienation is "a generic term used broadly to refer to a child who has been influenced to reject one parent, in extreme cases brainwashed or indoctrinated by an embittered/malicious other parent" (Kuehnle & Drozd, 2012; Saini, Johnston, Fidler, & Bala, 2012, p. 399). Parental alienation is very difficult to prove and to discern. Often the child is just reacting and has been so influenced that there is no boundary between the offending parent's opinion and the child's. Often a child loses out on years of relationship while this is happening. And the child may actually fear their parent, being afraid to ever relate normally to the parent who has been alienated. It is essential that in telling the co-parents about this they realize that when a parent alienates a child from the other parent, they are producing in their child a sense of abandonment, of not being loved by their parent. The parents need to know that this is generally destructive to the child, to grow up with a sense of abandonment. Abandonment is not easily overcome. Though producing abandonment may make the offending parent feel like they have won a battle for their child's heart, it really is destructive to the child's sense of safety and attachment. A sense of abandonment for any child is not easily repaired. It will affect every relationship that the child pursues for their entire lifetime. Poisoning a child against their parent is also a way of telling them that they are not of worth to the other parent. It will produce an underlying sense of shame, which is the belief that they are not worthy of love or belonging (Brown, 2015b). This alienation also denies the child the right to have their own opinion about their other parent and silences their voice. Again, no parent sets out to produce a sense of alienation in the child whom they love. But we need to raise their consciousness about the effects of their attitudes and actions upon their children.

12 **Blackmail:** When this pattern is used, the parents communicate their displeasure with their ex-spouse by communicating displeasure with their child. It is a way of retaliating against a spouse and using the child directly. An example would be to punish the child for something done at the other parent's home, rather than speaking with the other parent first. The child becomes the object of the parent's anger when the parent is really angry at their ex-spouse.

© 2018, *Working with Co-Parents*, Mary L. Jeppsen, Routledge

This is really hard for a child because they are powerless to change what occurs in either home. Often the child has no choice and no voice. Here they are truly being used as pawns in an effort to express anger and resentment to an ex-spouse. There needs to be a consistent set of standards in both homes, with consistent rules and consequences between the homes, so that this does not happen.

13 **Cutdown:** This happens when the child is exposed to direct put-downs of either parent in either home. This may have a direct negative effect on the child's identity development, as explained above. Studies show that children who are not exposed to negative comments about their parents, even if the parents are not harmonious, adjust more readily and successfully than their peers who are exposed to putdowns. Every custody agreement that I have read states that the parents are not allowed to speak negatively about their ex-spouse in the presence of their child. I have yet to meet a couple who has abided by this order on a regular basis. When I introduce this concept I emphasize that the child should not hear anything negative about the other parent, about the other parent's family or friends, or about any attachment figure associated with the other parent. I also express that the child should never see an eye-roll or a phone hang-up, or hear an exasperated sigh. The burden of self-control is placed on the divorced parents to protect their children from negativity related to their parents. Sometimes this means that the parents must set strict boundaries with their own parents and relatives who have sided with them in the divorce. Co-parents need to address this issue with their families and friends to assist their children in adjusting to the new life after divorce.

14 **Party Pooper:** When a parent criticizes the activities their ex chooses to participate in with their child, the child is put in a difficult position. Often inadvertently, a parent may have a negative or critical attitude about their ex-spouse. This attitude may permeate many comments made about them. Parents need to be careful that their negative attitudes toward one another do not spill into negative attitudes about the child's activities with that ex-spouse. When the child senses disapproval he or she may feel that they are not allowed to freely enjoy whatever experience he/she has had or is having with their other parent. The child may be embarrassed and/or angry because their parent has "rained on their parade". And this

© 2018, *Working with Co-Parents*, Mary L. Jeppsen, Routledge

may affect their further relationship with their other parent. One very important job of a co-parent is to foster a relationship between their child and their ex-spouse. In the short run this will produce a sense of security and trust in their child. In the long run, it will produce a sense of gratefulness in their child as they grow up and realize that in spite of hurt and pain, their parents decided to assist them in developing a good relationship with both of their parents. Again, this is a pattern where negative attitude and speaking will affect the child. Parents have a responsibility to encourage their children to have a good relationship with their other parent.

15 **Pay-Off:** This pattern happens when gifts, privileges, and promises are used as leverage for the relationship with the children. It can happen with children of any age. This is a lot like being a "Disneyland" parent but is more focused on material leverage used to gain loyalty and relationship. Here an insecure parent uses money, gifts, privileges, and promises to obtain the child's love and respect. In situations where there is an income differential (as in many divorce situations), this may also be very threatening to the ex-spouse. In divorce, spouses may be forced back into the workforce and may not have a secure income. And this practice may magnify the differential to the children and put them in a position of choosing the parent who can give them more. This may be very tempting, especially with teenagers.

Practicing pay-off may also give the child a false sense of power. The child may feel that they have power over the parent who does not pay them off, and the child may use the fact that one parent will give them more as a form of controlling the parent who can't. It will also teach the child that they can manipulate their parent to give them "stuff" in exchange for loyalty and even betrayal of the other parent. Obviously, a child who has played into this game will eventually regret their own actions, and they may even blame themselves rather than betraying the parent who has drawn them into it. For a child, there is no easy way to overcome such regret. Parents who co-parent need to know that the end game is not who wins the child's loyalty. It is about how the child grows up secure and happy. The parents need to be encouraged to change their focus. This is not a competition. It is a collaboration and a new lifestyle after divorce.

© 2018, *Working with Co-Parents*, Mary L. Jeppsen, Routledge

4   Out of Conflict into Compromise

The final psycho-educational session is on conflict resolution. This is a hard session as the co-parents likely do not do well at either communicating or conflict resolution. And some of the concepts that you introduce may be somewhat repulsive to them. Things like listening reflectively may be as attractive to them as remarriage. But it is necessary that they learn some conflict resolution skills. Even if there is a co-parenting plan in place, there will be conflicts in parenting. Both divorced and married couples have conflict as they parent together. For divorced people it is a bigger challenge because there is usually a breach of trust and trust is essential for parenting together. So, the emphasis needs to be trust within the boundaries of parenting and no farther. It is important to let the co-parents know that they are being courageous to even be in this therapy. Remember that we are attempting to develop new skills that will be the foundation for a lifetime of co-parenting. Hopefully by the fourth session the relationship between the co-parents will be somewhat de-escalated.

First there must be a review of previous concepts regarding trust, focusing on their relationships with their children and the effect of their interactions on the children. It must be reinforced that conflict is inevitable but must be entered into without the knowledge of the children. I begin by reminding the co-parents why they are here. Many of my clients are court-ordered; they are high-conflict couples who have not had a positive communication history. So, I remind them that their behavior has gotten them to this place and they need to move forward. I introduce this session as a session on resolving conflict. In any situation; whether after divorce or in a marriage, parenting is a high-conflict game. Even people who have been married for years engage in conflict over child-raising and discipline practices. How much more difficult is it to do this after a divorce? We are asking these parents to do an almost impossible task and we need to give them specific tools to use as they partner in parenting. We will introduce them to some very specific modes of communication, communication blocks, and a method of addressing difficult issues.

In addition, this session may also be used to bring up any huge blocks and unresolved issues that may be poisoning the parents' communication. This is delicate but should be treated as a necessary step. It should be emphasized that this is not post-divorce therapy, but huge blocks to communication need to be resolved. I encourage the couple to choose one, if any. Often these communication blocks are based on early misunderstandings and miscommunications. If we can assist the couple in resolving these, it may help them to move into a more constructive communication style.

The key components to conflict resolution are effective listening and effective communication. Our goal is to move from conflictual communication to mutual negotiation. The pathway to this more effective communication is effective listening and clear and kind communication. We begin by outlining the most common blocks to effective listening. At this point most co-parents recognize their inabilities to communicate well.

There are several ways to communicate in a conflict. I have chosen five basic stances that parents often have with one another as they co-parent and meet resistance. One stance is the competitive stance. This is prevalent with co-parents, especially when they are in custody battles—when competing parents are trying to one-up each other and prove who is better, more capable, or more loving. Conflict is seen as an opportunity to win rather than to work together. And often a parent's desire to win overshadows their ability to see what is in the best interest of their children. In extreme situations parents enlist their children to be part of the competition. This may take the form of spying and reporting on the other parent, asking them to testify in court, or colluding with them to form negative opinions about the other parent. The goal of winning overshadows the goal of having a good relationship and working together. If this stance continues, the hope of resolving real issues in a child's life is dashed for sure. And the child will be continually left in the middle without clear guidance.

The next common communication stance is that of avoidance. The parent chooses to avoid issues, refusing to work with the other parent. This may be easier on the uncomfortable parent, but it leaves the child with unresolved issues. If a child is asking about dating or permission for a school trip and parents refuse to communicate, one of two things happens. Either the child is left without an answer in limbo, and gives up their fight, or one parent makes a decision in spite of the other parent, thus placing the child in a position of wondering if they have their other parent's approval. The problem here is that two people cannot raise a child (no matter who has primary custody) without communicating and making some decisions together. This often happens when there is a big unresolved issue between parents. If there happens to be a large offense that the parents cannot overlook, this is when we take time to confront the issue and seek resolution. Sometimes resolution is possible. In the case of alleged domestic abuse there may be no resolution for the issue. That is when we encourage them to work together within a boundaried relationship, framed by the co-parenting plan, which they will author in the next sessions. The only way to completely avoid communication is the termination of parental rights and this is a very complicated and difficult process which most couples have no grounds to do.

Accommodating is another stance that is not helpful. I call this the "guilt trip". When accommodating, one parent acquiesces to the other without discussion. Basically they are saying, "You just do what you want and leave me here with no voice". This is an apparently effective way to avoid conflict, but it is really avoidance rather than compromise, and resentment will likely build to anger, and eventually cutoff will ensue in the co-parenting relationship. Again this attitude leaves the child without assurance of approval by both parents. It also will move the child to depend on the "decider" rather than on both parents. For a child this imbalance is a problem. They may develop a sense of abandonment and carelessness from the parent who acquiesces. As discussed in the first session, each parent has an essential voice that needs to be heard in the raising of their children.

Two habits of communication that can be helpful and constructive are collaboration and compromise. The parents share their opinions and collaborate on ideas or they listen and then compromise. This takes an amount of decisiveness, intentionality, and a bit of trust. Compromising means that you do something another person's way. This is counter to what most co-parents set out to do. But sometimes it is the most constructive solution. Collaboration is also counterintuitive for two people who have historically not gotten along. But sometimes it is necessary as both mother and father have essential wisdom for their children. And sometimes a combination of their collective thought is what is needed in decision-making. Our goal is to help these parents learn how they might resolve their differences and either compromise or collaborate in conflict.

After we have processed the most constructive stances for conflict, we need to lay a foundation for the basics of communication. The first building block of communication is effective listening. To listen effectively, co-parents need to recognize their own blocks to listening. There are several poor listening habits that will block effective listening.

Some common blocks to effective listening are:

1 **Mind reading**: When parents mind read they rehearse in their mind what they believe to be true about the other person. Understanding what the person is saying is overshadowed by a strong opinion about that person. We need to realize that it is impossible to know what a person is thinking. And it is very likely that the ex-spouse has changed and grown since the divorce.

2 **Rehearsing**: While another person is speaking, the parent is developing a comeback or response. This is a common practice with people. But it stands in the way of appreciating and understanding what is being communicated. If a person's attention is on a response, then they have likely missed a lot of what is being said.

3 **Filtering**: Teenagers are adept at filtering. When a person filters, they hear the bits and pieces of the conversation that they want to hear or expect to hear, and they reject what they don't want to hear. Again, these parents need to listen to each other because they will both have parental insight for their children. If a co-parent has a certain way that they understand their ex to be, this may create a filter where they hear what they expect rather than hearing the whole message.

4 **Judging**: Judging is related to mind reading but it is centered around assuming motive for what is being communicated. This can be a huge issue for divorced people who have been involved in litigation. Parents involved in custody battles may assume that their ex, with whom they are battling in court, will use what they say and do against them. Therefore, they will not be able to have an unfettered conversation with each other that might benefit their child. The parents must be encouraged to put their suspicions aside.

5. **Sparring**: Sparring is general argumentativeness. Some couples were argumentative when they were married and this carries into the co-parenting relationship. Sparring may be a habit of some people. But arguing is often futile and there is no resolution if people are arguing for the sake of arguing. First of all, it is harmful to argue in the presence of the children, and second, there is usually no conclusive outcome. When conflicts in parenting arise, resolution is the end goal. Co-parents who argue may never come to a conclusion and this leaves their child without any definitive direction.

6. **Being Right**: Some parents must be right, no matter what, and they cannot admit defeat. The conversation will not end until they are proven right. This, of course, is unproductive and unrealistic. Parents must be encouraged that they stand to lose nothing if they compromise with their ex over a parenting issue. As a matter of fact, they may well gain more respect from their child if the child is aware of the compromise.

7. **Derailing**: Derailing is very common after divorce. This is when any conversation can be turned into a character assassination of the other parent. Topics are twisted to point out parenting and character flaws. The point of the conflict conversation is often lost and no resolution is achieved. Derailing also adds fuel to the fire of negative talk about each other, and can be destructive for the children to witness.

These pitfalls can be avoided if the parents practice active listening skills. I introduce this segment by roleplaying a parent coming in to a conflict conversation and entering through a hallway, and checking their negative feelings at the door. I emphasize that when conflict arises or a decision needs to be made, they need to make an appointment with each other, meet in a safe place (preferably public), and limit their communication to the issue at hand. The key concept is respecting each other enough to take time aside for an appointment, and checking any and all negative feelings at the door for the duration of that appointment. The focus has to be on what's best for the children.

For this segment I borrow from Couple Communication (Miller, n.d.). In Couple Communication there is an emphasis on active listening and an awareness wheel is used to facilitate easy

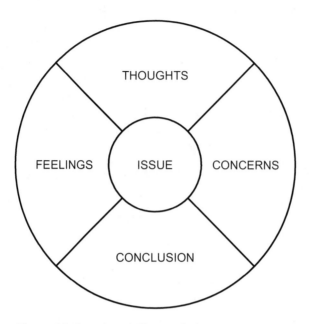

Figure 4.1 Steps in conflict resolution communication

communication over a topic(s). I actually use an interpretation of the awareness wheel to illustrate the concept of listening and taking turns speaking and responding. The communication circle is illustrated in Figure 4.1. The circle is used after a topic is chosen and an appointment is made to talk about that issue alone. This communication circle is less focused on communication of feelings and more focused on clear communication of opinions and concerns for divorced parents.

The next step is to train the co-parents in active listening. Active listening consists of listening to the other's thought, repeating that thought through paraphrasing the thought/statement, and asking for feedback. Each parent takes a turn at speaking their mind, emphasizing their feelings and thoughts about the subject as well as actions they think should be taken. The co-parents take turns until they have both heard each other, reflected back to each other what they have heard, and gotten feedback from each other. They will both have a chance to use their voice and share their thoughts and opinions. If this is repeated several times, hopefully conclusions will be drawn. After I have illustrated the process, I may ask the couple to practice this in the session with a topic that has been an issue for them. Remember that the issues here are issues regarding the children, not issues regarding hurt feelings or divorce, or money.

The second leg of effective communication is appropriate expression. This is generally more difficult for high-conflict co-parents. They likely have developed habits of hurt, sarcasm, avoidance, and meanness. In the session we need to acknowledge that if these are present it is normal, common, and nothing to be ashamed of. But we also need to point out that we are learning a new way to communicate, to give each other a clean slate. In appropriate expression the goal is clear, immediate, unfettered expression that is emotionally neutral. The parents must be reminded again and again of the idea of emotional neutrality. (Especially in a conflict conversation.)

In effective expression the parent is encouraged to use "I" statements. An "I" statement is impossible to argue with. It is also somewhat vulnerable. That's why it is effective. So, the parent is encouraged to observe and state the facts simply using "I" statements when communicating his/her needs and opinions. It helps to have the communication circle image for the co-parents as it provides a template for their conversation. Instead of the conversation going awry, there is a better chance that there will be constructive outcomes.

Then parents are encouraged to give a whole message rather than a partial contaminated message. Partial contaminated messages use withholding information and are often fraught with resentment and hurt. A well-placed reminder that divorce is a fact and that they are no longer a threat to each other will sometimes help parents to be willing to say what they are thinking and feeling about their children. Also, drawing a boundary around what is acceptable to speak with each other about is also helpful. Co-parents who set boundaries generally feel safer and more protected. When safer and protected, they are more likely to engage in open and honest communication. It is important to point out that their communication is about their children and their parenting. Nothing else is included in the list of acceptable topics of conversation with your ex! All conversations should be about the children. That is the safe zone.

So, in this session parents are taught the pitfalls to avoid in communication and they are given personal experience in practicing a form of effective communication. Then I remind them of the end goal of creating an effective business-type relationship where conflict is confronted constructively, for the sake of the children.

Personal Reflection

A couple was court-ordered for co-parenting. They could not communicate constructively. They were stuck in their resentment and hurt. I inquired about a blockage and the mother related an incident which occurred with the stepmother. It was interpreted hurtfully and was a major source of disrespect between the co-parents. Just voicing this helped Mom to become more expressive in the session and for Dad to be more understanding. The next session, we invited the stepmother to come in. They talked about the incident and it was actually a misunderstanding. It was resolved and the parents were able to move beyond the resentment. Often the "blocks" that are preventing clear and unfettered communication are based on misperceptions.

Handout for Session 4

The end goal for resolving conflict is to develop skills for effective communication: both for listening and expression. As co-parents you must set boundaries for your communication so that you limit your conversations to the children and parenting. If you do this, listening and speaking will be less threatening. Our goal is to collaborate and compromise in matters regarding the children.

Unhelpful forms of communication to avoid:

- Competing: You are not in a competition. You are parenting!
- Avoiding: You cannot parent together if you don't communicate.
- Accommodating: It is not helpful to lose your voice even if it seems more comfortable. Your children need your opinion too!

Blockages to good listening:

- Mind reading: You really don't know each other THAT well!
- Rehearsing: You may miss a nugget of wisdom.
- Filtering: Again, you may miss a nugget of wisdom.
- Judging: You are NOT your ex's judge.
- Sparring: Arguing will get you nowhere.
- Being right: Face it, you're not always right.
- Derailing: Every conversation is NOT an opportunity to criticize your ex.

Active listening consists of checking your feelings at the door, listening and paraphrasing, and asking for feedback. You deserve this and so does your ex when speaking about the children.

Successful co-parents respect each other as parents. They listen actively and communicate honestly using "I" statements. They put their own hurt on the shelf while communicating about the children for the sake of the children.

Commitments for conflict resolution:

How have we resolved conflict up to this point?

What is the most helpful (least uncomfortable) form of communication for us?

© 2018, *Working with Co-Parents*, Mary L. Jeppsen, Routledge

These are a few questions to consider as you develop a style of conflict resolution:

1 When we do not agree we will _____
   _____.
   (Compromise, give it time, put off the decision, make an appointment with a time and place to discuss)

2 We will allow _____ days/hours to consider an issue.

3 We will communicate by _____.

   (text, phone, email, face to face, carrier pigeon)

4 If we do not agree and a decision needs to be made, this is our contingency plan:

© 2018, *Working with Co-Parents*, Mary L. Jeppsen, Routledge

Outline To Use in Session 4

1 As you begin the session remind the couple that conflict resolution is likely not their forte.

2 Introduce the idea that conflict resolution has three parts: Listening, responding, and resolving issues.

3 Review the importance of their developing a template for conflict resolution so as to protect their children, and to make it easier for them to make decisions regarding their children.

4 Remind them that conflict is inevitable when raising children, for married and divorced people alike.

5 You may see a need to ask if there are any major blocks to their communication, any major offenses. This is the opportunity to bring these up and seek to resolve them. (Note that this is not marital therapy, but some resolution of offenses can happen.)

6 The key components of conflict resolution are effective listening and effective communication.

Discuss communication stances:

7 Competitive stance

8 Avoidant stance

9 Accommodating stance

10 Compromise

11 Collaboration

12 Point out that Compromise and Collaboration are the most constructive stances.

13 Introduce blocks to good listening.

14 **Mind Reading:** When parents mind read they rehearse in their mind what they believe to be true about the other person.

© 2018, *Working with Co-Parents*, Mary L. Jeppsen, Routledge

Understanding what the person is saying is overshadowed by a strong opinion about that person. We need to realize that it is impossible to know what a person is thinking. And it is very likely that the ex-spouse has changed and grown since the divorce.

15 **Rehearsing:** While another person, is speaking the parent is developing a comeback or response. This is a common practice with people. But it stands in the way of appreciating and understanding what is being communicated. If a person's attention is on a response, then they have likely missed a lot of what is being said.

16 **Filtering:** Teenagers are adept at filtering. When a person filters, they hear the bits and pieces of the conversation that they want to hear or expect to hear, and they reject what they don't want to hear. Again, these parents need to listen to each other because they will both have parental insight for their children. If a co-parent has a certain way that they understand their ex to be, this may create a filter where they hear what they expect rather than hearing the whole message.

17 **Judging:** Judging is related to mind reading but it is centered around assuming motive for what is being communicated. This can be a huge issue for divorced people who have been involved in litigation. Parents involved in custody battles may assume that their ex, with whom they are battling in court, will use what they say and do against them. Therefore, they will not be able to have an unfettered conversation with each other that might benefit their child. The parents must be encouraged to put their suspicions aside.

18 **Sparring:** Sparring is general argumentativeness. Some couples were argumentative when they were married and this carries into the co-parenting relationship. Sparring may be a habit of some people. But arguing is often futile and there is no resolution if people are arguing for the sake of arguing. First of all, it is harmful to argue in the presence of the children, and second, there is usually no conclusive outcome. When conflicts in parenting arise, resolution is the end goal. Co-parents who argue may never come to a conclusion and this leaves their child without any definitive direction.

© 2018, *Working with Co-Parents*, Mary L. Jeppsen, Routledge

19 **Being Right:** Some parents must be right, no matter what, and they cannot admit defeat. The conversation will not end until they are proven right. This, of course, is unproductive and unrealistic. Parents must be encouraged that they stand to lose nothing if they compromise with their ex over a parenting issue. As a matter of fact, they may well gain more respect from their child if the child is aware of the compromise.

20 **Derailing:** Derailing is very common after divorce. This is when any conversation can be turned into a character assassination of the other parent. Topics are twisted to point out parenting and character flaws. The point of the conflict conversation is often lost and no resolution is achieved. Derailing also adds fuel to the fire of negative talk about each other, and can be destructive for the children to witness.

21 Introduce the Couple Communication awareness wheel.

22 Practice effective listening on an issues, taking turns.

23 Review effective expression, emphasizing clear and unfettered responses. Tell them about checking their feelings at the door when they are discussing difficult issues.

24 Encourage them to make an event and appointment to discuss conflictual issues or big decisions either by phone, in person, or through text and/or email.

© 2018, *Working with Co-Parents*, Mary L. Jeppsen, Routledge

5 Including Step-Parents in the Process

With many divorced couples, step-parents are not yet present, but with many others there is at least one step-parent who is alongside one of your clients trying to encourage and "be on their side". You can assume that every step-parent is seeking to heal and help their spouse. They are invested in their spouse and are for the most part defending them. It is their right and privilege and it is essential for the divorced person to have good support. Because step-parents are such a big part of the parents' lives and because they are also trying to navigate parenting with the step-child, it is essential to include them in the co-parenting process.

However, you must be very careful to create the scenario that is best suited for the co-parents you are working with. There are several things to take into consideration. You must remember that your clients are the co-parents, and that it is your responsibility to create as safe an atmosphere as possible for both of them. Including a step-parent in any session where both parents are present should always be done with the consent and foreknowledge of each parent. If, for any reason, that co-parent is very uncomfortable with the step-parent, then meeting alone with the step-parent should take place before an "all hands on deck" meeting. This is quite possible if one parent is remarried and the other is not. Never create a scene where a co-parent feels ganged up on or left out. Your purpose may be served best to meet with step-parent and spouse alone to introduce the step-parent to the process and the concepts of co-parenting, and to gain insight into their concerns. Remember that co-parenting is essentially the two biological parents in a business-type relationship. Step-parents can be seen as consultants and helpers in the process. Often step-parents can soften the relationship between the co-parents, especially if you as a therapist enlist them in this process.

The main goal to accomplish with step-parents is to allay any fears or suspicions they may have of their spouse meeting alone with their ex for eight sessions, and to get them on board to encourage the spouse in the co-parenting process. I have had two clients who were court-ordered to have co-parenting with the step-parent present because the judge discerned that the step-parent would be a calming influence in the room. This proved to be quite successful.

Several scenarios are possible with step-parents. Step-parents may take part in all of the sessions. In this case, a step-parent is listening on the sidelines while the co-parents hash things out. In many cases stepmom or stepdad may relate better to the co-parent than the ex-spouse. This is positive but also may distract the ex-spouse from taking their full responsibility as a co-parent. In some high-conflict situations it may be necessary to allow the step-parent to be the main communicator. But I would only recommend this if all else fails.

Step-parents may come for sessions alone without their spouse. This is helpful to ascertain any issues that the co-parents may be unwilling to share. The step-parent may have first-hand experience and may be able to give you useful information which will help you to address issues in co-parenting. At least one session where therapist and step-parent are alone or with their spouse is recommended so that the therapist can begin to build trust and safety with the step-parent. It is important to note that the parenting of a child or children is a group effort and everyone involved in the parenting needs some awareness of what is happening in the co-parenting counseling.

Step-parents may come with the co-parent or spouse. I think this is a helpful scenario. This situation enables the co-parent to express support of the step-parent and vice versa. It will also give you an idea of the type of parental influence the step-parent has. In this session it is advisable to talk about the role of a step-parent. This role is one of supporter, and never of a major disciplinarian. The step-parent has a unique position in a child's life. They are intimately involved and yet they are not the major authority figure. They have the privilege of speaking into a child or parent's life in a non-threatening manner. A step-parent can make or break the co-parenting process. It would behoove the co-parenting counselor to recognize this essential resource.

Another option is to have no step-parent involvement at all. When I began to work with co-parents, I did not include step-parents unless they specifically requested it. My experience tells me that every scenario in which a step-parent was involved in either part or all of the co-parenting process was more successful. And when the step-parent was not involved, there was more likely to be extended animosity on the part of one or both co-parents. Often hurt is transmitted to the step-parent by the opposite co-parent. Co-parents may be threatened by the step-parent as well. It is important to get the principal people in the child's life in the same room to work through these negative feelings to allay one another's fears.

It is important to note and to remind co-parents that step-parents are next in line to be mother and father to the children if the biological parent passes away. It would behoove a parent to get to know the person who will be assuming their parental responsibility. It is also important in the parenting process for the co-parent to support their child's relationship with their step-parent. Children need to know that all of the adults in their lives are working together for their good. This is a best-case scenario for developing a secure base.

Personal Reflection

I worked with a set of co-parents early in their divorce journey. Two years later when they had both remarried, they were court-ordered to return to complete the co-parenting process. This couple was "stuck" in their negative communication patterns. They had been to court several times and they continued to be suspicious and to attempt to micro-manage the other's parenting practices. They had not completed a parenting plan, and had no intention of truly working together. We began to work on a plan and they were not progressing. They continued to pick at each other and they were very negative. I suggested that I meet their new spouses. This turned out to be a stroke of genius because the spouses were reasonable and calm. I met alone with each couple to define the co-parenting process and the goals of making a co-parenting plan. Thereafter the two couples were present for making the plan. The atmosphere was totally different. Each co-parent seemed to feel safe in the presence of their spouse and the spouses took their role of peacemaker and advocate seriously. We completed a plan and decided that the major communication would be between one co-parent and one step-parent to alleviate stress on the co-parenting relationship. This was a collaborative decision,

(continued)

(continued)

made by the four individuals. And it has worked well. This was a unique situation. It is important to realize that each set of co-parents and step-parents is different and the communication plan should be tailor-made for each set of co-parents.

Homework Reflection Questions

1. What is my relationship like with my co-parent's spouse?

2. Am I willing to develop a relationship with my ex's spouse to enhance my co-parenting effectiveness?

3. What boundaries do I feel most comfortable setting with the step-parent of my child?

6   Each Parent Needs a Voice

This work of co-parenting counseling is a balancing act. Trying to stay neutral in a situation which often lends itself to taking sides is a task that not many therapists relish. In some ways the therapist experiences the same pressure as the children of divorce when faced with the fighting or disagreement or hostility of the co-parents. This session is designed to enhance the therapist's connection with each parent and to assist the therapist in understanding the needs of each parent for safety and security as they go forward to make a co-parenting plan together. I find that having an individual session after the psycho-educational piece is most helpful because it has allowed the co-parents to have time to digest the concepts of emotional neutrality and cooperation as well as consider their effect on the children. It seems more fruitful and timely to wait to meet alone with them, although most co-parents will pressure you to meet with them and hear their story at the outset. Hold your ground. I explain that I want them to know the concepts and goals that we are working toward before we meet. In very few cases seeing parents alone prior to the psycho-educational piece might be suggested. One scenario might be when domestic violence or abuse is in the couple's history. It is important to know this at the outset of therapy and to set boundaries in the therapy room, knowing that you as a therapist are responsible for the safety and wellbeing of your clients in your office.

The most important piece of the individual session is to join with the parent and hear their story and their concerns. Hopefully by now there is a relationship that has developed with a certain measure of trust. Hopefully you have exemplified neutrality to the co-parents and have been fair as you have processed ideas during the psycho-educational piece of the therapy. During this individual session it is not your job to defend the other parent. It is your job to listen and take note of any and all concerns that each co-parent may have. Often this session is a time when a co-parent shares their own parenting agenda with you. They may also plead their case for custody or extended visitation. I find this session to be somewhat difficult because I must side with the client in my room, and support them with empathy, even if I have heard negative stories and scenarios from their ex-spouse previously. It is the ultimate balancing act, for sure. I try to communicate how important it is to move on, to work together, and I assure them that as we go forward into making a plan, I will do my best to advocate for them. I do this with both parents. And, yes, it is possible to advocate for both of them. Remember that the co-parenting plan is to be established for the good of the children. It is my job, and yours, to combine both parents' concerns into a cohesive document which will meet the parenting needs of the children.

Another consideration to remember is that as we move forward into making a co-parenting plan, our aim is NOT to change any agreed-upon court order, but to serve the children with both parents' interests in mind.

In most cases the individual session is a time when I take copious notes on the parents' hopeful outcomes. I also use the time to encourage the parents to work together, and try to ascertain what I need to emphasize in the planning session to help the couple get over any non-communication hurdles.

Some questions to ask during the individual session:

1   How are things really going as you co-parent?

2   What changes would you like to see in your co-parenting relationship?

3   What are your biggest concerns going forward?

4   What type of visitation are you aiming at? (This is likely in a court order, but asking this question really helps reveal the balance of power in the co-parenting relationship that can be addressed in the next session.)

5   How do you think your children perceive your relationship with your co-parent?

6   Are you willing to compromise?

7   (If a step-parent is involved.) How does your spouse get along with your co-parent?

Outline to Use for Individual Sessions

Some questions to ask during the individual session:

1 How would you honestly describe your co-parenting relationship at this point?

2 What changes would you like to see in your co-parenting relationship?

3 What are your biggest concerns going forward?

4 What type of visitation are you aiming at? (This is likely in a court order, but asking this question really helps reveal the balance of power in the co-parenting relationship that can be addressed in the next session.)

5 How do you think your children perceive your relationship with your co-parent?

6 Are you willing to compromise with your co-parent?

7 (If a step-parent is involved.) How does your spouse get along with your co-parent? How can I help facilitate this relationship?

© 2018, *Working with Co-Parents*, Mary L. Jeppsen, Routledge

7 Developing the Co-Parenting Plan

The climax of co-parenting therapy is the development of a thorough and collaborative co-parenting plan. This plan serves to provide a safety net for the co-parents and a template that they can use as they parent in separate houses. I explain to the co-parents that in a marriage there are differences and conflicts over parenting. In marriage the parents' love and respect for each other is a safety net when differences cause problems. Co-parents have no safety net. If there are differences there is likely conflict, and there is no concrete fallback when there is conflict. I explain that we are creating the co-parenting plan as a safety net for them. Therefore, the co-parenting plan is detailed and outlines all the parenting practices and modes for communication and decision-making so that both co-parents can feel a measure of safety with each other in their respective parenting roles. At the outset of therapy I remind the co-parents that this is our end goal. I ask them to keep a growing list of the topics that they want to address in the co-parenting plan.

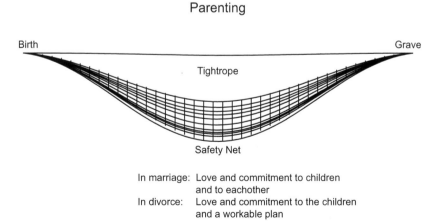

Figure 7.1 The co-parenting plan provides a safety net for the divorced couple

In most cases there is a court order in place for many practices after divorce. But in some cases parents come to co-parenting counseling prior to the actual divorce proceedings. So, this co-parenting plan can be something that the couple agrees upon prior to court. I explain to them that this is their chance to develop their own practices and agree upon important topics. I also explain that the co-parenting plan is NOT a legal document. Rather, it is an agreement between them that they can submit to their lawyers. There have been cases where this plan or parts of this plan have become a part of a court order. In any case this is an opportunity for the co-parents to discuss pertinent issues and resolve some potential conflict.

There are several topics that are always addressed. Some may seem obvious but in divorce nothing is obvious or without emotion. It is important to address even the most trivial issues to provide the co-parents with a sense of emotional safety.

Issues are as follows.

Visitation

Visitation has probably been addressed by the court. If the co-parents are not terribly contentious, it may be pertinent to address if they would like any changes. I do not address this if there is an active custody suit, unless I have been asked by the court to do so. If there is no final divorce decree it is important to address this. No matter who has custodial parental rights, there needs to be an agreed-upon schedule of visitation. There are many different situations represented when visitation is addressed. There is standard visitation, which is court-initiated. And there are several options for non-standard visitation. It is my viewpoint that children need as much of both parents as possible. So, half and half time visitation may be a preference. But if a couple is NOT getting along, such visitation might wreak emotional havoc for the child, who may not feel like they belong anywhere. So, in high-conflict custody cases, I leave this to the court. In cases where there is delineated custody and the parents have been sent to me for communication issues, I do ask preferences and discuss if the couple would prefer a change. It is important to note that the co-parenting plan is not a legal document so stating a preference does not make that preference legal.

Pick Up and Drop Off

We address when and where exchange occurs and what issues the co-parents have with this. We address the place, time, and contingency plan for late arrivals. We also address who will pick the child up, if others are allowed to do this.

Phone Calls

Because phone calls are usually part of the court order, we address their frequency and timing. I address the importance of respecting the other parent's time, and being careful not to intrude upon this time. I also address the need for the child to have both parents have a presence in either house. If there is no problem with intrusiveness I recommend a nightly bedtime call by the non-custodial parent. This should be a very short call, two minutes or less, at an agreed-upon time. If the co-parent tends to intrude upon the other co-parent's time, we set a regular time weekly, which is agreed upon by both parties. If the parents say that the child has their own phone and can have complete freedom, I always suggest guidelines, which protect bedtime and the dinner hour. Both parents need to respect each other's privacy and time with their children and balance that with their desire to be accessible to their child.

Electronics

Video games, screentime, TV time, and phone boundaries are all covered in the co-parenting plan. Both parents must discuss what types of games the children are allowed to play and how much screentime they are allowed, as well as which websites and television shows are allowed. I always counsel parents to use parental controls because the average age for a child to access porn is presently 10 years old. It is important that both parents are on the same page for the child's standards. Phones should be put up at the same time in each home, if that is a request of the parents. Both parents must be aware of what the children are involved with electronically.

Standards of Behavior

Children should have the same expectations in both households. Therefore, parents must discuss what is important to them concerning the behavior of their children. I ask what they value and what they would like to instill in their children. Usually this is where both parents come to realize that they are more alike and on the same page. We then list their priorities.

Discipline

Just as standards must be a common thread in both households, discipline should also be consistent for the child. Here we outline what the discipline procedure will be and what currency the parents might use to discipline. The child must know that their rules are generally the same in both homes, and the disciplinary procedures are the same as well. Of course there may be some variation, but it will be variation on the same theme. A child should not be spanked in one household and not in another. A child should not be allowed to eat Fruit Loops every day in one household and only oatmeal in the other. The parents need to be somewhat consistent without being identical.

Activities

Deciding upon a child's activities is a major issue. Here we develop standards and a procedure to follow. For example, a couple may decide together that each child is allowed only one extra-curricular activity per semester. Then they develop a procedure as to how to choose this activity. Usually the child's interests are paramount. Then there is a discussion between parents, and a decision is made. We also discuss how these activities are paid for. Parents have many different ways to handle this. Some say that child support should cover it. Others divide activities and say that each parent can decide the activity that happens on their watch and pay for it. Others divide sports and arts among themselves. And others split everything down the middle. The important thing is to decide a method so that there is as little disagreement as possible in the future.

Holidays

Normally the court-ordered visitation schedule outlines the procedures for holidays, but in some cases parents want to be more creative for the sake of their children. Here we discuss any changes and also policies about asking for different visitations and times at holiday time. Many parents have glitches when family comes into town irregularly. Here we outline the timeframe in which they need to ask for a change and how to make sure the other parent has compensatory time.

Summer

The court order normally outlines summer visitation. However, as children get older there may be changes due to camps and other activities.

These policies need to be addressed. When to decide upon camp, how to navigate compensatory time, and how to navigate longer summer vacations all need to be addressed. Remember that this process is somewhat grueling but will alleviate pressure later for the co-parents.

Medical Decisions

This is normally outlined in a custody agreement but I have found it to be a source of contention for some co-parents. Provision must be made for both parents to receive medical information at the least and a procedure for both notification and involvement in medical decisions should be outlined.

Communication

It is likely that the co-parents have been sent to you for communication issues. Therefore, a workable and safe method of communication should be agreed upon. Most co-parents come to me and they are either texting or e-mailing. I always suggest that they use an online app designed for co-parents. If an app is used it protects both parents from feeling intruded upon by the other co-parent. In most online apps, there is a function for e-mail, messaging, and a common calendar. I call it a one-stop shop. I encourage the co-parents to decide upon a response time for issues and I encourage them to access the app once a day at their own convenience. This eliminates much daily stress of having to answer an ex during work hours or the dinner hour. And it gives both co-parents the freedom to communicate when it is convenient for them, without fear that they will be interrupting their ex. Using an online app is also efficient because everything pertaining to the children can be accumulated in the same space. Both parents have access to a common calendar so that they can be aware of school activities and appointments, and bills, pictures, and documents can be uploaded. Best of all, parents can access this place at their convenience, when they are mentally prepared. We also make provision for texting and calling in the event of a real emergency or when there are last-minute changes of plans. The online app is a great insulator for co-parents.

Non-Negotiables

I like to ask each parent if there is any non-negotiable that they would like the other parent to be aware of. Some parents have said things like: "Little Jonny will never be in the presence of Uncle Vinny", or "Suzie will always wear a helmet when riding her bike". Many parents have no non-negotiables but they should have an opportunity to express these.

Teen Issues

Parents of teens have more to discuss. We outline ages for dating, curfews, when and if they will meet boyfriends and girlfriends, if the teens can go in cars with the opposite sex, overnight policies, when to buy a car and who will pay for it, college plans, evaluating teen friends . . . All of these may be discussed and if decided upon will alleviate pressure for the co-parents. It is interesting that when I discuss teens with most co-parents, they usually agree with each other more often than not.

Significant Others

Here we discuss how and when the co-parents will introduce significant others to the children. I usually ask them to tell each other prior to introducing the child. But I make it clear that this is merely a warning and not a vetting process.

Step-Parents

The most important thing to communicate to co-parents is that the children need their permission, both spoken and unspoken, to have a good relationship with step-parents. Often children feel guilty for loving the new mother or father. It is important that co-parents encourage these relationships. I also emphasize that the step-parent's role is supportive and that the step-parent should never be the major disciplinarian in a child's life.

Agreement Not to Litigate and Report

At the end of every co-parenting plan I include a statement that says that the co-parents agree not to litigate or report their ex-spouse until they have first consulted a mediator or mental health professional. I include this because one aim of this therapy is to help lighten the load of the Family Court System, which is generally overloaded.

The next step is to type up the agreement and send it to the co-parents, asking if any changes need to be made. The final draft can be sent to the court or lawyers if you have complete releases of information from both parents.

Outline to Use in Development of Co-Parenting Plan

1. Visitation:

2. Pick up and drop off:

3. Phone calls:

4. Electronics and screentime:

5. Standards of behavior:

6. Discipline:

7. Activities:

8. Holidays:

9. Summer:

10. Medical decisions:

11. Communication:

12. Non-negotiables:

13. Teen issues (curfew, cars, dating, jobs, etc.):

14. Significant others:

15. Step-parents:

16. Other specific issues of interest to parents:

17. Agreement not to litigate or report without counsel:

© 2018, *Working with Co-Parents*, Mary L. Jeppsen, Routledge

8 The Final Family Session

A family session(s) at the end of co-parenting therapy can be an incredibly healing experience for both parents and children. When children are old enough to be aware of the issues between Mom and Dad, the family session can mark a new beginning with new habits and more security and comfort for the child. I use a combination of Directive Play Therapy and Emotion-Focused Family Therapy in this session, depending on the age and maturity of the children. It is a shared experience where both parents are connecting with their children. This is often something that has not happened for the children in a very long time. And it is normally encouraging for the children.

During the last session of the co-parenting plan I prime the parents about this session. Here I emphasize the importance of providing a safe place in the session for the children. I tell them, as I would in Emotion-Focused Family Therapy, that this is an opportunity for them to really listen to their children. It is a time where their normal patterns of relating, which may be unhelpful, are recognized and interrupted, and they take the stance of listener. I encourage them to really listen to and connect with their children's feelings, resisting the urge to defend themselves. We talk about emotional connection, and empathizing with their children's feelings and experiences. The purpose of the session is to give the children a voice and an opportunity to establish a deeper emotional connection with both parents in the same room.

If the children are younger, I use play therapy interventions, which are less verbal, and we emphasize the shared experience and the processing of that shared experience. The focus continues to be on establishing or reestablishing emotional connection with both parents in the room. Note that this is not a substitute for the child's individual therapy, if they are in therapy. Rather, it is the inclusion of the children in the new co-parenting process.

Meeting the children can take several different forms. Sometimes I will have an individual session with the children to establish a rapport and to explain the process to them. I usually meet them as a group if there is more than one child. I explain that I have been meeting with Mom and Dad to help them to get along better as they parent, and to help them be better parents after divorce. The children are generally very in tune and grateful for my work with their parents. I join with them, and establish a conversation centered around their experience of their parents parenting. Then I tell them that this is an opportunity for them to tell their parents their concerns. I emphasize that their parents are trying very hard and want to listen to them.

Either after a brief meeting or after a full session with the children, we bring the family together. Sometimes this is the first time that the parents and children have all been together in a room without others since the divorce. In my experience the children are generally more comfortable than the parents. I introduce the session as a time where we are going to communicate our feelings and establish a new way of relating.

With teens I might use a family play genogram-type experience to break the ice. This intervention uses miniatures (from the sand tray). The family members are asked to pick 1–3 miniatures to represent each family member. When they have each finished picking their representations, we go around the room telling what they picked and why. This often gives way to relationship discussion, and personal communication of feelings. I use Emotion-Focused Family Therapy skills to focus the family members on creating and reforming emotional bonds, always emphasizing their love for each other. This is where the Emotion-Focused Therapy Practice of "catching the bullet" (Greenberg & Johnson, 2010) will be very useful. When a therapist "catches the bullet" they take a potentially negative comment and reframe it into a statement about love and connection. For instance, a teen might be angry and lash out with words to their parent. The therapist would reframe that and say, "Your relationship with your parent is so important to you that it's very upsetting. You are fighting for a better relationship with your parents. That must be so difficult for you". In Emotion-Focused Family Therapy there is a positive focus and everything is interpreted through an attachment lens. In other words, our job in this final session is to enhance emotional attachment and reestablish emotional bonds.

A play intervention is not always used in this session. With older children I may just ask the children to say what they need to say to their parents about the divorce and the co-parenting situation. Often teens will say that they do not want to be caught between their parents. Parents have been prompted to apologize, and to listen, and these moments can be extremely precious for the parents and children.

With younger children I use the sand tray and art interventions. One play intervention which is very useful for a family with younger children or a family with mixed ages is the Color Your World/Feeling Heart Activity. In this intervention the family members are given paper and asked to draw a large heart on a piece of paper. I provide crayons or markers. Then I ask them to choose five colors to match five feelings that they have had about their family (or parents or co-parenting or the divorce). They then choose their feelings and write them next to the heart in a kind of legend. Then I ask them to color these feelings into their heart as much as they have them and where they have them. After the family members have finished coloring in their hearts, they are asked about each area, from biggest to smallest. What causes this feeling? When do they have this feeling? This intervention is especially effective with younger children who do not have as much verbal prowess as their teen counterparts. The intervention provides a safe place for the sharing of feelings and this often gives way to a deeper emotional connection.

So the family session establishes a common experience. The parents have an opportunity to communicate to the children that they have made a plan for parenting together and that they will be working together. This is also a time where parents can apologize to the children for their own mishandling of the co-parenting relationship after divorce. It is also a way for the parents to maintain some sort of accountability to their children. I always joke with the children that they can call me if their parents begin to reestablish old habits. The parents may choose to go over their co-parenting plan with the children as well, informing the children that both of them will be working together, with consistent discipline and rules between both homes.

If the family needs further family therapy, this may be the beginning of a long-term relationship. Sometimes the court will order more therapy for families after divorce.

Personal Reflection 1

The most beautiful family session that I have experienced in this context was with a family that had just decided to divorce. They were establishing their rules of engagement when they came to me. They had two young children, a preteen and an elementary-school child. After completing the co-parenting plan, this couple

(continued)

(continued)

continued to wonder about what custody arrangement would be best considering the ages of their children. For the family session we did a Feeling Heart. The children expressed fear that they would not see enough of each parent, and the parents expressed the same feeling. The family was united in their desire to be together as much as possible. It was beautiful to see Mom and Dad listen to the concerns of their children, and their children's desire to be with them both. The experience softened the parents as they discussed custody arrangements, and it comforted the children to know that Mom and Dad had the same concerns. This intervention provided the parents with the information they needed as to whom the children needed to see the most (in this case both). And it prevented anyone from asking the children the dreaded question of who they wanted to live with. It was a very comfortable and safe way to communicate uncomfortable feelings with one another. Play interventions often give space for difficult conversations.

Personal Reflection 2

With an older child, Mom and Dad were asked to listen to the concerns of two teenagers. Both teens expressed their feelings of loving both parents (who had been competing for two years). Both teens also asked that they would never again be put between their parents. Both parents cried and asked the children for forgiveness. They dropped their lawsuit for a change of custody, and they are getting along well because they were able to connect emotionally with their children's experiences and feelings. This emotional bond with their children made all the difference in their relationship as co-parents. Often when parents engage in legal proceedings the emotional bond and humanity of the ex-spouse and their children are overshadowed by the legal battle. Using the family session to refocus on emotional connection often reminds parents that they are to be looking out for the best interests of their children.

9 Therapeutic and Ethical Challenges

Conflict-intensive couples are extremely difficult to work with. As mentioned previously, many couples that come for co-parenting help are court-ordered because the court has no recourse but to order some type of change. So, the involvement of court and lawyers automatically complicates the therapeutic process. Ethical issues such as confidentiality and maintaining neutrality are of utmost importance. Releases of information must be obtained by both parties for lawyers and also the court, if the court requires a report. A court order does not necessarily mean that you as a therapist are free to communicate with the court or the ordering judge. Ethically you must have a release from both parents to speak with anyone regarding your work with the co-parents.

In my work, I do communicate often with most ad litem attorneys. The court in Arkansas puts a lot of responsibility upon the ad litem attorney to represent the interests of the children. These attorneys are normally interested in what happens in co-parenting therapy, and they will often look to the therapist for clues as to what decisions are in the best interests of the children. If a therapist is solicited by a lawyer who represents either parent, it is important that a release is obtained from both parents. Conversations with lawyers for either side should be carefully worded to promote compromise and good will between the parties. In Arkansas where I practice, there are no parental evaluators so custody battles end up being informed by therapists, lawyers, and sometimes psychologists. The position of the therapist is strategic because often we are the most neutral parties involved and clients feel safest with us. Just as we have been encouraging our clients to maintain a neutral stance, we must also. However, if a couple has been court-ordered and a judge expects a report, we must be honest about our prognosis. I have written judges (with the consent of both parties) about court-ordered clients and been honest, stating that they did not do well, that they should expect them to be back in court, or that they do not do well parenting together. Sadly, not all couples are willing or ready to allow themselves to parent together.

Another occupational hazard in this work is the likelihood of a client reporting an ethical violation against us. This work is continually challenging for co-parents. And as discussed previously, we are dealing with a lot of personal hurt and offense. As we are guiding the co-parents to get along better, their resentment and anger may lodge against us, especially if we challenge them to change or compromise more than they are comfortable with. Two years ago I received two letters of accusation sent to my Board. Thankfully, I had done nothing unethical. But it was frightening and a complicated process to answer each accusation and to work with my liability insurance lawyers. Even if we are not at fault, we are obligated to answer our accusations, and to engage a lawyer for our own protection. I am actually thankful that I have experienced this because it has allowed me to know what the process is in my state, and it has made me more aware of the Code of Ethics and judging my own work in light of the ethical code. Whenever we are juggling the emotions of two offended people we run the risk of being accused of being an offender ourselves.

I see myself as an advocate for children in this work. At the outset of the work, I have never met most of the children whom their parents represent. But I am passionate to help them end up with the best parents they can have. I am also convinced that every parent is doing their best in the situation they are in. Divorce is such a painful and emotionally draining experience. If I can come alongside a set of parents and help and encourage, I can make their children's life easier. I tell parents at the beginning that I am not on either of their sides, but I am on their child's side and that I want to deliver the best parents I can to these kids. I make it clear that I believe that what they are doing is really hard. And I tell them that I respect their willingness to be vulnerable enough to meet together with me.

This work is not outwardly rewarding. Co-parents will not call and tell you how well they are doing after they complete the therapy. They have too much on their plate adjusting to their own life changes. Often only one parent will have been engaged in the therapy. I get responses from clients who tell me that they appreciated the therapy but nothing has changed because their ex-partner was disengaged. This can be discouraging. Often we never see the family again. It is in-the-trenches work, where we put out and do not have enough of a therapeutic change to feel good about what we did. However, in some cases we do. Those cases give encouragement for the others.

This work is not sexy. It is not a new creative therapy. It is more like being in charge of the ball at a tennis game, running to keep the ball in the air while the two players are refusing to aim right. It is exhausting. It requires attentiveness, compassion, empathy, patience, confrontation, and constant reframe. This work is not for the fainthearted.

But this is necessary work. Co-parents need help. Divorced parents need help. Children of divorce need advocates. I would invite therapists who are adventurous and compassionate to engage in this work.

Further Study

Dr. Jeppsen is interested in therapists who would be willing to be faithful to the template and engage clients in a before-and-after survey.

If you are interested in contributing to further study using this method of co-parenting therapy, please contact Dr. Mary Jeppsen at drmary@freshroots familycounseling.com.

You can also contact her through her website at drmaryjeppsen.com.

Releases and permissions will be copied and maintained by the therapist who does the work. You will be given access to an online survey to use during the timeframe of the study.

Permission to Release Information for Study

I hereby give permission for Dr. Mary Jeppsen to use information gained from this survey in an academic study pertaining to co-parenting. I understand that there is little chance of harm to myself or my family since all responses are anonymous and will be used only for study purposes. I agree to answer each question to the best of my ability and to submit the questionnaire without any identifying characteristics online.

Name

_____

Date

_____

Bibliography

American Psychological Association. (n.d.). Marriage and divorce. Retrieved from www.apa.org/topics/divorce.

Baker, A. J., & Fine, P. R. (2014). *Co-parenting with a toxic ex: What to do when your ex-spouse tries to turn the kids against you.* Oakland, CA: New Harbinger Publications.

Beckmeyer, J. J., Coleman, M., & Ganong, L. H. (2014). Postdivorce coparenting typologies and children's adjustment. *Family Relations, 63*(4), 526–537. doi:10.1111/fare.12086.

Bloomfield, H. H., & Kory, R. B. (1993). *Making peace in your stepfamily: Surviving and thriving as parents and stepparents.* New York, NY: Hyperion.

Bonds, D. D., & Gondoli, D. M. (2007). Examining the process by which marital adjustment affects maternal warmth: The role of coparenting support as a mediator. *Journal of Family Psychology, 21*(2), 288–296. doi:10.1037/0893-3200.21.2.288.

Bowlby, J., Miesen, B., & Munnichs, J. (1986). *John Bowlby: Attachment, lifespan and old-age.* Deventer, Netherlands: Van Loghum Slaterus.

Brown, B. (2014). *The gifts of imperfection: Let go of who you think you're supposed to be and embrace who you are.* Charleston, SC: Instaread Summaries.

Brown, B. (2015a). *Daring greatly: How the courage to be vulnerable transforms the way we live, love, parent, and lead.* London, UK: Penguin Books Ltd.Brown, B. (2015b). *Rising strong.* New York, NY: Spiegel & Grau.

Daughtry, T. (2011). *Co-parenting works! Helping your children thrive after divorce.* Grand Rapids, MI: Zondervan.

Deal, R. L. (2006). *The smart step-family.* Minneapolis, MN: Bethany House.

Emery, R. (2016, July 26). Two homes, one childhood. Retrieved from www.psychologytoday.com/blog/divorced-children/201607/two-homes-one-childhood.

Farber, E. D. (2013). *Raising the kid you love with the ex you hate.* Austin, TX: Greenleaf Book Group Press.

Feinberg, M. E., & Kan, M. L. (2008). Establishing family foundations: Intervention effects on coparenting, parent/infant well-being, and parent-child relations. *Journal of Family Psychology, 22*(2), 253–263. doi:10.1037/0893-3200.22.2.253.

Flowers, J. (2016). *The conscious parent's guide to coparenting: A mindful approach to creating a collaborative, positive parenting plan.* Avon, MA: Adams Media.

Floyd, F. J., Gilliom, L. A., & Costigan, C. L. (1998). Marriage and the parenting alliance: Longitudinal prediction of change in parenting perceptions and behaviors. *Child Development, 69*(5), 1461. doi:10.2307/1132278.

Gaies, J. S., & Morris, J. B. (2014). *Mindful co-parenting: A child-friendly path through divorce.* North Charleston, SC: CreateSpace Independent Publishing Platform.

Gillespie, N. N. (2004). *The stepfamily survival guide.* Grand Rapids, MI: Revell.

Greenberg, L. S., & Johnson, S. M. (2010). *Emotionally focused therapy for couples.* New York, NY: Guilford Press.

Groenendyk, A., & Volling, B. (2007). Coparenting and early conscience development in the family. *The Journal of Genetic Psychology, 168*(2), 201–224. doi:10.3200/gntp.168.2.201-224.

Grohol, J. M. (n.d.). Encyclopedia of psychology. Retrieved from http://psychcentral.com/encyclopedia.

Hoberock, B. (2014, June 5). New Oklahoma law requires class before many divorces. Retrieved from www.tulsaworld.com/homepage-latest/new-oklahoma-law-requires-class-before-many-divorces/article_be443a5a-db28-5f84-81a4-86186ca20d7e.html.

Jamison, T. B., Coleman, M., Ganong, L. H., & Feistman, R. E. (2014). Transitioning to postdivorce family life: A grounded theory investigation of resilience in coparenting. *Family Relations, 63*(3), 411–423. doi:10.1111/fare.12074.

Johnson, Sue. (2013). *Love sense.* New York, NY: Little, Brown and Company.

Kids First Center (n.d.). Intensive co-parenting course. Retrieved from www.kidsfirstcenter.org/for-parents.html#coparenting.

Kreider, R. (2004). *Living arrangements with children: 2004.* Current Population Reports. Washington, DC: U.S. Census Bureau. Retrieved from www.census.gov/prod/2008pubs/p70-114.pdf.

Kuehnle, K., & Drozd, L. (2012). *Parenting plan evaluations: Applied research for the family court.* New York, NY: Oxford University Press.

Light, J. (1995). Coparenting with your ex. *Essence, 25*(11), 118.

Markham, M. S., & Coleman, M. (2012). The good, the bad, and the ugly: Divorced mothers' experiences with coparenting. *Family Relations, 61*(4), 586–600. doi:10.1111/j.1741-3729.2012.00718.x.

McHale, J., Kuersten, R., & Lauretti, A. (1996). New directions in the study of family-level dynamics during infancy and early childhood. In J. McHale & P. Cowan (Eds), *Understanding how family-level dynamics affect children's development: Studies of two-parent families.* San Francisco, CA: Jossey-Bass.

McHale, J. P., & Lindahl, K. M. (2011). *Coparenting: A conceptual and clinical examination of family systems.* Washington, DC: American Psychological Association.

Miller, S. (n.d.). The awareness wheel. Retrieved from http://couplecommunication.com.

Morrill, M. I., Hines, D. A., Mahmood, S., & Córdova, J. V. (2010). Pathways between marriage and parenting for wives and husbands: The role of coparenting. *Family Process, 49*(1), 59–73. doi:10.1111/j.1545-5300.2010.01308.x.

Owen, J., & Rhoades, G. K. (2010). Reducing interparental conflict among parents in contentious child custody disputes: An initial investigation of the working together program. *Journal of Marital and Family Therapy, 38*(3), 542–555. doi:10.1111/j.1752-0606.2010.00215.x.

Pollet, S. L., & Lombreglia, M. (2008). A nationwide survey of mandatory parent education. *Family Court Review, 46*(2), 375–394. doi:10.1111/j.1744-1617.2008.00207.x.

Saini, M., Johnston, J. R., Fidler, B. J., & Bala, N. (2012). Empirical studies of alienation. In K. Kuehnle & L. Drozd (Eds), *Parenting plan evaluations: Applied research for the family court* (pp. 399–441). New York, NY: Oxford University Press.

Stahl, P. M. (n.d.). Parallel parenting for high conflict parents. Retrieved from http://citeseerx.ist.psu.edu/viewdoc/download?doi=10.1.1.555.3667&rep=rep1&type=pdf.

Sullivan, M. (2013). Coparenting: A lifelong partnership. *Family Advocate, 36*(1), 18–20.

Wallerstein, J. S., Lewis, J., & Blakeslee, S. (2000). *The unexpected legacy of divorce: A 25 year landmark study.* New York, NY: Hyperion.

Weissman, S., & Cohen, R. (1985). The parenting alliance and adolescence. *Annals of the American Society for Adolescent Psychiatry, 12*, 24–55.

Index

abandonment xiii, xvii, 18, 41, 48, 56, 61
abuse 1–2, 39, 54, 61, 77
accommodating stance 61, 67, 69
acting out 17–18, 20, 29, 38, 41, 53, 55
active listening 22, 31, 63–65, 67
activities 84, 87
ad litem attorneys 93
adjustment xvi, 15, 16, 28
adolescents *see* teenagers
adoption 5
affairs 10, 40, 55
alienation 41, 47–48, 56
anger 5, 8, 9; accommodating stance 61; blackmail 42, 48, 56–57; children's 17, 20, 21–22, 25, 26, 29, 31, 41, 55; towards therapist 94
anxiety 17; infants 19, 28; litigation 38, 53; separation 20, 25, 29
apps 85
argumentativeness 35, 50, 63, 70
art interventions 91
attachment ix, xi–xii, xviii; Emotion-Focused Family Therapy 90; enhancing xvii, xix, 90; impact of abandonment on 41, 56; infants 19, 25, 28; interrupted xiii; search for secure 17
attorneys 93
avoidance 60–61, 65, 67, 69
awareness wheel 63–64, 71

balancing act 77, 78
behavior, standards of 83, 87
being right 63, 67, 70–71
betrayal 37, 46, 48, 52
bitterness 5
blackmail 41–42, 48, 56–57

Blakeslee, S. xii, xiv, 15
blame, internalization of 18
boundaries to communication 65, 67
Bowlby, John xi–xii
Brown, Brené 19
business analogy 8, 14, 16

camps 84–85
"catching the bullet" 90
choosing sides 8, 17, 21, 30–31; set-ups 40, 47, 55; teenagers 22–23, 26, 32; wish bone 39–40, 47, 54–55
co-parenting, definition of xiii–xiv
co-parenting plans 75, 81–87, 91
collaboration 44, 58, 61, 67, 69
Color Your World/Feeling Heart Activity 91
communication xv, 33–59; avoidance 60–61; blackmail 41–42, 48, 56–57; blocks to 60, 62–63, 66, 67, 69–71; co-parenting plan 81, 85, 87; conflict resolution 60; cutdown 42, 48, 57; Disneyland parents 37–38, 47, 52–53; effective 63–65, 71; habits 33–34, 44, 49; I Spy game 37, 46, 51–52; "I wish" fantasies 36, 46, 51; pain game 34–36, 46, 49–50; party poopers 42–43, 48, 57–58; pay-off 43–44, 48, 58; property rights 38–39, 47, 53–54; set-ups 40–41, 47–48, 55–56; step-parents 75–76; wish bone 39–40, 47, 54–55
competition xii–xiii, 18, 60, 67, 69
compliance 40, 55
compromise 61, 63, 67, 69, 71, 78, 79
confidentiality 2, 93

conflict xi, xiii, 59, 81
conflict resolution 59, 60, 64, 67–69, 82
consistency 38, 42, 48, 53, 57, 84, 91
counselors 38, 53
countertransference 4
Couple Communication 63–64, 71
court cases ix–x, xi, 4; personal reflection 23–24; testifying in court 39, 53–54, 60; *see also* custody battles; litigation
court-ordered couples xv, 1–2, 59, 66, 74, 93–94
court orders 78, 79, 82, 93
criticism xvii, 35, 46, 50; party poopers 42–43, 48, 57–58; recurring opinion 44; *see also* negative comments
custody agreements 8, 42, 57, 85
custody battles ix–x, xi, xiii, 1, 92; competitive stance 60; judging 62, 70; position of therapist 93; *see also* court cases; litigation
cutdown 42, 48, 57

damage, emotional 15
de-escalation xi, xv, xviii, xix, 59
Department of Human Services (DHS) 35, 46, 50
derailing 63, 67, 71
Directive Play Therapy 89
discipline 37–38, 47, 52–53, 84, 87, 91
Disneyland parents 37–38, 47, 52–53
divorce, prevalence of ix
Drozd, L. 41, 56

electronics 83, 87
Emery, Robert E. xii
Emotion-Focused Therapy ix, xi, xviii, 89, 90
emotional damage 15
emotional neutrality 6, 7, 8–9, 12, 14, 65, 77
emotions x, 16; children 19, 22, 26, 31–32; final family session 89, 91, 92; "I wish" fantasies 36, 51; limited 9, 14; self-denial 23, 26, 32, 40–41, 55
empathy xviii, xix, 5, 89, 95
ethical issues 93–94
extended families 17

family history 3–4, 5, 9–10, 14, 18–19
family members 5, 42, 57
fantasies 20–21, 25, 29–30, 36, 46, 51

Farber, Edward David x, 8
Feeling Heart activity 91, 92
filtering 62, 67, 70
final family session 89–92
forgiveness 44, 92

games 83
genograms 3, 5, 14, 90
gifts 43, 48, 58
grandparents xiii, 5
grief 5, 10, 12, 14
ground rules 2
group programs xi
guilt 22, 26, 32, 86; guilt trips 61; I Spy game 37, 46, 52; "I wish" fantasies 36, 46, 51

hatred 8, 9
history 3–4, 5, 9–10, 14, 18–19
holidays 84, 87
homes 16–17
hurt xiii, xviii, 9, 10, 65, 66, 75

I-COPE program xv
I Spy game 37, 46, 51–52
"I" statements 65, 67
"I wish" fantasies 20–21, 25, 29–30, 36, 46, 51
identity development 40, 47, 48, 55
income differentials 43, 58
infants 19, 25, 28
informed consent 2
insecurity xiv, 8, 47
isolation xii, 41, 55

Johnson, Susan xvii–xviii
judging 62, 67, 70
judgment 19

Kuehnle, K. 41, 56

lawyers 93, 94
Lewis, J. xii, xiv, 15
Lindahl, K. M. xiii–xiv
listening 21–22, 59, 60, 69, 71; active 22, 31, 63–65, 67; blocks to 62–63, 67, 69–71; final family session 89, 90; step-parents 74
litigation 1, 2, 4, 92; co-parenting plan 86, 87; pain game 34–35, 49; property rights 38–39, 47, 53–54; *see also* court cases; custody battles
loss xii, xiv, xv, 5, 12, 14
loyalty xiii, 22, 26, 32, 43–44, 48, 58

manipulation 43, 48, 58
McHale, J. P. xiii–xiv
medical decisions 85, 87
mind reading 62, 67, 69–70
mistrust xviii, 3, 5
misunderstandings 60, 66
money 43, 48, 58

negative appraisal xvii
negative comments 21, 30, 42–43, 57–58, 63, 71, 90
negative patterns xvii–xviii, 34; blackmail 41–42, 48, 56–57; cutdown 42, 48, 57; Disneyland parents 37–38, 47, 52–53; I Spy game 37, 46, 51–52; "I wish" fantasies 36, 46, 51; pain game 34–36, 46, 49–50; party poopers 42–43, 48, 57–58; pay-off 43–44, 48, 58; property rights 38–39, 47, 53–54; recurring opinion 44; set-ups 40–41, 47–48, 55–56; wish bone 39–40, 47, 54–55
neutrality: emotional 6, 7, 8–9, 12, 14, 65, 77; therapist's 2, 4, 93
nightmares 20, 25, 29
non-negotiables 85–86, 87

online apps 85

pain 10, 18; pain game 34–36, 46, 49–50
parent education xiv–xv, 2; *see also* psycho-education
parental alienation 41, 47–48, 56
parentification of children xii, 18, 28
parenting styles 37, 38, 52, 53
partners 17, 86, 87
party poopers 42–43, 48, 57–58
pay-off 43–44, 48, 58
phone calls 83, 87
pick-up and drop-off times 35–36, 46, 50, 82–83, 87
plans 75, 81–87, 91
play therapy x, xi, 89, 91, 92
powerlessness 38–39, 42, 47, 53, 56–57
prevalence of divorce ix
privacy 83
privileges 43, 48, 58
promises 43, 48, 58
property rights 38–39, 47, 53–54
psycho-education xv, 2, 3, 33, 59, 77
psychosomatic complaints 21, 25, 30

puberty 22, 26, 31
punishment 34–36, 46, 49–50
putdowns 42, 48, 57

recurring opinion 44
regression 19, 25, 29
rehearsing 62, 67, 70
rejection xiii, xvii
reporting 35, 46, 50, 86, 87
repression 22, 32
resentment 5, 8, 9, 66; accommodating stance 61; blackmail 42, 57; partial contaminated messages 65; towards therapist 94
resilience 16
respect xviii, xix, 6, 12
responsibility: children's sense of 17, 24, 28; parental 38, 43, 47, 48, 58, 67
role models 5, 14, 23

safety 6–8, 12, 17; attachment xi–xii; co-parenting plan 81, 82; first sessions 2; impact of abandonment on 41, 56; parent's need for 77; safe space 36, 51; toddlers 20, 25, 29
sand trays 91
sarcasm 65
schedules: changing 35, 46, 50, 84; co-parenting plan 82
secrecy 19
secure base xiv, 6, 14, 17, 20, 29
security 6–8, 16, 37, 52; attachment xi–xii; fostering a relationship between child and ex-spouse 43, 58; parent's need for 77; toddlers 20, 25, 29
self-control 42, 57
self-denial 23, 26, 32, 40–41, 55
separation anxiety 20, 25, 29
set-ups 40–41, 47–48, 55–56
shame 19, 22, 26, 32, 36, 41, 51, 56
sides, choosing 8, 17, 21, 30–31; set-ups 40, 47, 55; teenagers 22–23, 26, 32; wish bone 39–40, 47, 54–55
significant others 86, 87
silence 19
sparring 63, 67, 70
standards of behavior 83, 87
step-parents 5, 17, 73–76, 78, 79, 86, 87
stonewalling xvii

storytelling 18, 28
structure, lack of 37–38, 47, 52–53
summer visitation 84–85, 87

teenagers 22–23, 26, 32; co-parenting plan 86, 87; filtering 62, 70; final family session 90, 92; pay-off 43, 58
television 83
testifying in court 39, 53–54, 60
therapeutic relationship xix
timelines 3, 19
toddlers 19–20, 25, 29
toxic relationships xiii
trauma xiv–xv

triangulation xiv–xv
trust xviii, 59, 61, 74; *see also* mistrust

visitation 35, 50; co-parenting plan 82, 87; Disneyland parents 37, 52; holidays 84; questions to ask parents 78, 79; summer 84–85, 87
voice, parent's 77–79

Wallerstein, J. S. xii, xiv, 15
wanted-ness 9
wish bone pattern 39–40, 47, 54–55
withdrawal xiii, 22, 26, 31